Annie Proulx's
The Shipping News

CONTINUUM CONTEMPORARIES

Also available in this series:

Forthcoming in this series:

· **ANNIE PROULX'S**

The Shipping News

A READER'S GUIDE

ALIKI VARVOGLI

CONTINUUM | NEW YORK | LONDON

2002

The Continuum International Publishing Group Inc
370 Lexington Avenue, New York, NY 10017

The Continuum International Publishing Group Ltd
The Tower Building, 11 York Road, London SE1 7NX

www.continuumbooks.com

Copyright © 2002 by Aliki Varvogli

All rights reserved. No part of this book may be reproduced,
stored in a retrieval system, or transmitted in any form or
by any means, electronic, mechanical, photocopying, recording,
or otherwise, without the written permission of the publishers.

Printed in the United States of America

Library of Congress Cataloging-in-Publication Data

Varvogli, Aliki.
    Annie Proulx's The shipping news : a reader's guide / Aliki Varvogli.
        p. cm. — (Continuum contemporaries)
    Includes bibliographical references.
    ISBN 0-8264-5233-7 (alk. paper)
    1. Proulx, Annie. Shipping news.   2. Newfoundland—In literature.
I. Title. II. Series.
PS3566.R697 S48 2002
813'.54—dc21
                                                                    2001047832
    ISBN 0-8264-5233-7

Contents

The Novelist

Annie Proulx's advice to aspiring writers is "to spend some time living before you start writing", and her own unusual writing career and meteoric rise to fame seem to confirm the wisdom of these words. Proulx had her first novel published when she was 57 years old, and before she turned sixty she had already gained a series of prestigious literary awards, as well as a wide readership and great critical acclaim. In the 1970s, having completed the course-work towards a PhD, she left university without finishing her thesis. By 2000, she had gained not one but three honorary degrees, from the Universities of Maine, Toronto and Montreal. Meanwhile, she made history by being the first woman to be awarded the P.E.N.-Faulkner Award for Fiction in 1993, and by the end of 1994 she had also won the National Book Award for Fiction, the *Irish Times* International Fiction Prize, and the Pulitzer Prize for Fiction.

These days, Annie Proulx is compared to great American writers — most notably Ernest Hemingway and William Faulkner. Yet at an age when both of those literary greats had already produced their best work, Proulx's writing career consisted of non-fiction titles such as *The Fine Art of Salad Gardening* (1983) and *The Complete Dairy Foods Cookbook: How to Make Everything from Cheese to Custard in Your Own Kitchen* (1982). Even though the writer is famously reticent when it comes to her personal life, she has talked to interviewers about the circumstances that led to this dramatic change in her fortunes, and a brief look at her life will also help to shed some light on the extraordinary progression from writer of how-to manuals to award-winning author.

THE NON-FICTION YEARS

E. Annie Proulx (the E. stands for Edna, and Proulx rhymes with true) was born in Norwich, Connecticut in 1935, and she grew up in New England and North Carolina. Her French Canadian father had started out as a bobbin boy in a textile mill, and worked his way up to become vice-president of the company. His work commitments meant that the family had to move frequently, but even so he was often absent from home, absorbed in his work. "I suspect my intense and single-minded work habits stem from his example", says Proulx, who often wakes up at 4 am and starts writing in the house she built herself. Her mother was a keen story-teller, an amateur naturalist and a painter, and Proulx attributes her attention to detail, her painstaking descriptions of surfaces and textures, to her mother's painterly eye. She explains how her mother taught her to see everything: "from the wale of the corduroy to the broken button to the loose thread to the disheveled mustache to the clouded eye". From her mother she also inherited a love for storytelling: "There is a strong tradition of oral storytelling in my mother's family and, as a child, I heard thousands of tales and adventures made out of nothing more substantial than the sight of a man digging clams, an ant moving a straw, an empty shoe". Proulx was the eldest of five daughters, and this, she says, may explain why the main characters in her fiction are men: "I always wanted a brother and I liked the things that men did; when I was growing up, women didn't go skiing, or hiking, or have adventurous canoe trips, or any of that sort of thing. I felt the lack of a brother whom I imagined could introduce me to the vigorous outdoor activities that my sisters were not particularly interested in. If you live in a woman's world and that's all there is, the other side of the equation looks pretty interesting. For me the invented male character perhaps puts the brother I didn't have into a kind of reality".

Proulx studied history at the University of Vermont, and then did an MA at Sir George Williams University (now Concordia University). She stayed at the same institution for a doctoral degree, but after completing her coursework requirements she gave up her studies in order to provide for her three sons. She has been married and divorced three times; two of her marriages she describes as "terrible", and she has remarked that she "had a talent for choosing the wrong people". She remains, however, very close to her children. She thanks her three sons in the acknowledgements for both *Postcards* and *Accordion Crimes*, and *The Shipping News* is dedicated to them. A further thanks to Muffy Clarkson which appears in *Accordion Crimes* refers to her previously estranged daughter, with whom she is now happily reconciled, and *Accordion Crimes* and *Close Range: Wyoming Stories* are dedicated to all four children.

Having abandoned her studies in the mid-seventies, Proulx moved to Canaan, on the United States-Canada border, and the question of how to make a living while staying in a remote, rural area, seemed to be answered by writing. Before she turned to fiction, she wrote journalism as well as a series of how-to manuals on cooking, gardening and wine-making. Even though this work was undertaken mainly in order to "put meat and potatoes on the table", the subjects she wrote on also reflected her own interest in rural life and self-sufficiency: "What interested me at this time was the back-to-the-land movement—communes, gardening, architecture, the difficulty of maintaining a long, dirt-road driveway. Not only could I solve some of those problems in real life and observe what people were doing to make things work in rural situations, I could write about them and make some money. So I did. And I made a damned good living for a number of years doing this". After Canaan, she spent many years in Vermont, in a house she built herself, and more recently she has moved to Wyoming. She consistently chooses to live away from big urban centres, in places where she can pursue her outdoor interests, which include skiing, canoeing, fly-fishing, hiking and bird hunting.

Her chosen lifestyle, so untypical of an American female author, indicates someone who is not entirely at home giving interviews or undertaking tours to promote her novels. Even though she is not a recluse, and has been involved in promotional tours, book signings and literary festivals, the fame that writing has brought her continues to make her feel a little uneasy; she says that this exposure "gives you a very odd, meat-rack kind of sensation". "I think that writers are much more comfortable standing in the corner of the room watching other people and not putting on the party hat and doing the dance themselves". Above all, however, she dislikes the trappings that come with literary fame because she does not want to be distracted from writing: "At first I couldn't say no and I did a lot of things that I shouldn't have", she explains. "When you get through with travel and hassle and rushing about and shaking people's hands, that "one hour" usually translates into three days. And if you're working on a piece of writing, once three days are torn out it can be quite difficult getting back to where you were before the interruption came. It is possible to make a living not through writing but through celebrity appearances. Some writers do it. But writing is utterly absorbing for me, and I resent anything that pulls me away from it". Elsewhere, she has put it more succinctly: "I'm desperate to write. I'm crazy to write. I want to write".

This urge to write fiction and tell stories has a lot to do with her earlier journalistic career: "After 19 years of writing tedious non-fiction", she says, "all these stories were just bottled up inside of me". And even though non-fiction provided a good source of income, "gradually this kind of thing became more and more boring, and my interests changed. I began to move towards fiction for intellectual stimulation". This move toward fiction, Proulx says, owes a lot to her reading habits. She describes herself as an "omnivorous, greedy reader", and thinks that reading was a crucial part of her apprenticeship: "It's probably natural for readers to move into writing, and that's essentially what happened to me". It is curious, however, that a writer who admits that she found her vocation through reading books is so reluctant to acknowledge any literary influences, or talk about her work in relation to other contemporary writers. She is known to have described *Independent People*, the 1945 novel by Icelandic Nobel laureate Halldór Laxness as one of her top ten favorite books of all time, but beyond that she leaves it to the critics to draw parallels or infer influences. For her part, she admits that she reads "for pleasure" 98 percent of the time, but she almost contradicts herself by adding that she certainly takes note of "other writers' technical virtuosity, style, and daring literary risks".

PROULX'S FICTION: SOME MAJOR CHARACTERISTICS

Proulx may be reluctant to discuss literary influences, but she is happy to talk about where she gets her inspiration from as well as revealing, through the unusually extended acknowledgements that preface each of her books, the type and scope of research she has undertaken. "For me, the strongest influences are the varied landscapes and bare ground of the hinterlands, rough weather and rural people living lives in the pincers of damaging isolation, ingrained localisms, and the economic decisions made by distant urban powers", she wrote in her *New Yorker* essay "Big Skies, Empty Places", effectively summing up the nature of her fiction. As we shall see in the next chapter, her comment about the economic decisions made by urban centers of power is a very significant one. Because of her attention to detail in creating believable microcosms, it is easy to assume that her fiction shows little interest in the wider socio-economic forces that shape the world her characters inhabit. However, Proulx's novels are neither apolitical nor oblivious to the unseen factors which have an impact on rural life. Moreover, the harshness of the landscape she describes, and the miseries that so often blight the lives of her characters, are in themselves indications that she is not indulging in "pastoral nostalgia", to use her own phrase. In highlighting the effect, she is indirectly drawing attention to its causes.

In addition to finding inspiration in rough terrain and rural lives, Proulx also admits her fascination with language, especially idiolect, specialized language and regional variations. When she was writing *The Shipping News*, she says she slept with a copy of the *Dictionary of Newfoundland English* as well as *The Ashley Book of Knots* which provided the epigraphs for each chapter. In "Big Skies, Empty Places" she writes: "I am influenced by words and the chewiness of language, the specialized phrases and names that have come out of human work and travel through the landscapes—like 'dry-ki,' the deadwood on river sandbars. Old work words are falling into the pit of obsolescence as we abandon the labor of hands and bodies. [...] I collect dictionaries of work and trades, of dialects and phrases". Once again, in addition to highlighting her interest in the texture of words, this passage also reminds the reader that language is political in that it reflects, in this instance, practices which are becoming obsolete due to economic changes.

Over the years, Proulx had written a number of short stories, and these were collected in *Heart Songs* in 1988. When her contract for that book was being drawn up, her editor suggested that it include a novel as well; "And I just laughed madly", says Proulx, "had not a clue about writing a novel". Later, once *Heart Songs* had been published and received favorably by critics, the idea of following it up with a novel was put to her again. This time, she did not dismiss it: "I sat down, and within a half-hour, the whole of *Postcards* was in my head" she says. Needless to say, that magical half-hour during which the novel was conceived was the culmination of years of experience, and of a long and varied apprenticeship. Proulx's are not the kind of novels that can be written overnight, and the reader only has to look at the acknowledgements in each novel in order to see why.

The very practice of including an acknowledgements page is more often associated with academic and other non-fictional works, although some writers do thank family members, editors, and foundations which provided funding for their writing. In her first novel, *Postcards*, Proulx thanks all of the above, but she also acknowledges the help she received from librarians in New Hampshire and Wyoming. For *The Shipping News*, she thanks among others the Canadian Coast Guard Search and Rescue unit, a member of staff from the Massachusetts Horticultural Society Library who "confirmed some obscure horticultural references", as well as fishermen, loggers, and people she met and talked to casually during her trips to Newfoundland. The list grows even longer in *Accordion Crimes*, where she thanks everyone from music specialists and accordion experts to friends who provided hard to find records, tapes and CDs, and others who offered advice on ski routes and stuck garage doors. For *Close Range*, the acknowledgements reveal that she flew on a plane in order to get a feeling for the landscape from above, talked to people about sheep farms, and travelled to the Cowboy Poetry Gathering in Elko, Nevada. These pages should, perhaps, be read with a pinch of salt. Even though there is no reason to doubt the sincerity of the gratitude expressed in the acknowledgements, the excessive and meticulous listing of so many people who helped the author with her research verges on parody. Writers are often asked how they write, where they get their inspiration from, where they find the stories they tell, and maybe Proulx's extensive credits are meant to suggest that no amount of factual information can fully account for the genesis of a work of art. Given that these extensive lists appear in the beginning of the book, Proulx should perhaps be understood as a magician who reveals the secrets of her art, and then goes on to trick the reader all the same.

According to the author herself, her attention to detail stems not so much from her days of writing manuals, as from her earlier academic research coupled, of course, with a natural curiosity about the world: "It became second nature to me to explore how and where things were done", she says of her research, and what is reflected in her writing is the result of "serious academic hours in libraries and archives and an inborn curiosity about life". It is often said that every writer's first novel, no matter how well disguised, is to some degree autobiographical, but it is hard to see how this could apply to *Postcards*. Proulx's interest in research, along with a vivid imagination and an extraordinary degree of empathy, have allowed her to avoid the advice she most hated receiving: "write about what you know"; she calls that "a constipated, navel-picking approach to the world that does not encourage growth of the imagination, nor interest in dialect and languages, nor appreciation of the idiosyncracies and behaviour of others, nor refreshing the eye with travel, nor the useful exercise of putting oneself in another's skin".

In addition to helping her re-create wholly accurate worlds enriched with detail, this amount of research has also created a kind of writing which bears little resemblance to the writer's own lived experience. This fact testifies to the powers of the imagination, which Proulx calls "the human mind's central life strategy". "For many people — for me, certainly — the life of the mind, the realm of the imagination, is a more brilliant and compelling one than the world we live in. [. . .] Imagination is the central pivot of human life". This coupling of painstaking research and the author's imagination has produced fictional works which seem realistic in that they are both plausible and seemingly authentic. Proulx writes about the poor, the dispossessed. Her books are always set in the country, usually within farming communities, depicting the little-known and rarely represented lives of people away from the big cities that have dominated twentieth-century America's literary map. Everything, from each of her character's mindset, to their unfamiliar speech patterns, to descriptions of the changing weather, to the finer points of laying traps for wild animals, seems entirely convincing. However, as we shall see in the next chapter, Proulx's brand of realism is often deceptive, and each of her books contains sufficient clues to remind the readers that what appears to be a representation of a real world is, in fact, the creation of a fictional one. In all of her writing, the use of elaborate narrative techniques and the vocabulary which brings her characters to life blur the lines between reality and fiction.

Both Proulx's life style and her chosen themes and characters seem far removed from what has been constructed as a typically female sphere, and the author has indeed attracted criticism for not writing specifically about female experience. Writers, critics and literary theorists who have made the case for "women's writing" being studied as a separate, discrete entity, do have various valid points. They argue that specifically female experience is largely absent, under-represented or even mis-represented in fiction, thus alienating a large section of the reading public, as well as leaving many stories untold. In addition, the large majority of critics, intellectuals and academics who decide what constitutes "good" literature have for a long time been predominantly male, a fact which has influenced aesthetic judgement. However, Proulx believes that men and women are the same deep down, and it is those similarities that interest her more than the differences. In 1997, she called for an end to "women's writing" in an essay she published in *The Observer*. "The differences between men and women are certainly there", she wrote, "physical and psychological, tied to a million years of hunting/child-bearing specialisation, but the differences seem paltry in comparison to the similarities shared by both sexes, the adult humanness of both men and women and the shared emotional spectrum". Given these fundamental similarities, women should not be expected to choose themes relating to what may be thought of as predominently female experience, she argued, nor is it legitimate to talk of "women's writing" in relation to an author's writing technique: "Having a vagina and breasts instead of penis and testicles does not order subject, form, narrative nor anything else unless the author wishes it so", she explained. Proulx also historicized her argument by pointing out that her ability to break free from the constraints of gender has a lot to do with historical and social changes which have taken place in the twentieth century:

To separate and harp on the differences in an antithetical way is somewhat reactionary in light of the immense shift in gender role and identification that has occurred in this century, from control of child-bearing, increasing economic and political power of women, surgical sex changes and the increased recognition of lesbian and gay presence in the general population. If the information age has done nothing else, it has made us aware of the complexities of categories, the infinite possibilities of sub-heads and cross-indexing.

Time for Mighty Casey to Turn His Back

Mighty Casey comes to bat, 114 years after Ernest Lawrence Thayer's famous poem.
Casey's now making $6.7 million a year while batting .237. And he don't sign no stinkin' autographs:

There was ease in Casey's manner as he stepped into his place.
There was pride in Casey's bearing and a smile lit Casey's face.
And when responding to the cheers, he lightly doffed his cap,
No stranger in the crowd could doubt 'twas Casey at the bat.

Ten thousand eyes were on him as he rubbed his hands with dirt.
Five thousand tongues applauded when he wiped them with his shirt.
Then while the writhing pitcher ground the ball into his hip,
Defiance flashed in Casey's eye, a sneer curled Casey's lip.

And now the pitch came hurtling through the humid August air,
And Casey stood a-watching it—heading for his hair.
Close by the sturdy batsman the forkball spinning sped,
"This ain't right, I'm walking. Blame the union," Casey said.

From the bleachers bright with people, there rose a muffled roar,
Like the beating of the storm waves on a strange and distant shore.
"If you walk, then we'll walk, too," said the fans, they sounded certain.
"Go out and leave us hanging, we won't be back; it's curtains."
The team owners, they weren't worried, they'd been through this before.

Heck, they faced this in 1980, then again in '94.
We have issues fans don't understand, the masses won't get them, mostly.
Payroll taxes and other things, our billions, we guard them closely.

"Fraud!" cried the maddened players, "There's fraud across the land."
Our forefathers went through this for us, Curt Flood, he took a stand.
If we let owners get their way, they'll take away our millions,
They'll take away our steroids, they'll take away our children.

The sneer hadn't fled from Casey's lips, the teeth were clenched in hate,
He cursed the owners' egos, he pounded on the plate.
"A salary tax and other things, you'll see what we're about.
We'll fight this to the final cent; we're striking!" he did shout.
And when Casey turned to see them, the faces in the stands,
The mothers and the brothers, his aunt, his Uncle Stan,
No one was there but ushers—a peanut guy, devout,
"Nuts! Nuts! Nuts! to all of you, the fans have all walked out."

Chris Erskine's column is published Wednesdays. He can be reached at chris.erskine@latimes.com.

declarations such as, say, shirts proclaiming "I'm with stupid," which simply render conversation moot.

"Creating conversation—real conversation—is our mission. We wanted to do something to combat all the negativity," says Friedler, who earned both a bachelor's degree in business and an MBA at Loyola. "I wanted to do something that elevated life, love and consciousness. . . . So one night, 4 a.m., we just said: Let's do it."

Principal figures behind the Charizmatic line include, left, Osamu Nishimura, Ricardo Santos, Alex Ross, Freddie Friedler and Zen Ni

In Order to See the First Pitch, 'Operation: Parking

Drive Time

By MARY McNAMARA
TIMES STAFF WRITER

We took the kids to a Dodger game and we went by a way that was so sneaky and traffic-free that I'm not even going to mention it. As we were scooting through the entrance kiosk, we congratulated ourselves on achieving, at long last, tension-free travel. And then we hit the parking lot.

At 4:45 last Sunday, spread out beneath the slight rise of the Elysian Park entrance, the parking lot of Dodger Stadium glittered menacingly. This is anthropomorphism of the most unrestrained kind—a parking lot is not capable of any action, much less one with intent. But that is what it did. It glittered. Menacingly.

Up one row and down the other, windshields and windows shone flat silver like the bellies of a thousand anchovies washed up on the beach, and the symbolic portent was just about the same. Something evil was rising, something we thought we could outrun, outthink, outmaneuver. But, of course, we could not. We were going to have to face down the inevitable specter of Parking Lot Anxiety.

For me it begins as a churning drop in the stomach, followed by a breathlessness that makes me gulp for air a bit like a goldfish eating and causes my remarks to come in tommy-gun, declarative bursts that include a lot of direct appeals to the Almighty. I quickly realize we are never going to find a parking space, that if we get out of this alive it will be more than we deserve, that we were fools, *fools*, to ever think we could go to a Dodger game/Disneyland/Costco/the state fair when clearly we should have stayed at home playing endless games of Candy Land and Red Light/Green Light like families are supposed to.

Then I notice that it's not just cars that fill this parking lot, it's also people. Strings of people, many of them hand-holding families and all headed in the same direction. Now my skin starts to itch, and the top of my head heats up so I can visualize the air above it shimmering. I'm an American, I pay taxes, I bought my ticket, I can certainly take my children to a baseball game/theme park/seasonal event with everyone else if I want to.

But we had better hurry the heck up and find a parking space or all the good stuff—the seats and churros, short lines and commemorative pins, not to mention the lifetime supply of money and medical supplies and the free passes to heaven—are going to be gone.

This is about the time I begin giving urgent, pointed advice to my husband if he is driving, or to the cars around me if I am driving. You can imagine how pleasant that is for everyone involved.

When we at last find a parking space, I spring into action like a blood-frenzied panther. In one motion, I turn off the car, the car, lean into the c the kids out of the car husband is still unlatchi belt. I grab the diaper b stroller and the sweatshi hats, thrust small feet find naked baby dolls the whole mess ever fo there were alarms sour the boat listed starboar in oilskin sou'westers lifeboats into the icy sea

All around me people and cars add themselve and my mouth fills wit ish taste of dread. We just as the man wh gate of the ballp Fair—who in my min bles the man with t hat who tried to tur

The essay concluded with the wish for a "post-feminist stage in American women's writing", where women are free to choose both subject and voice as freely as men are. Her fictional output to date clearly indicates that such an option can be both viable and desirable.

PROULX'S OTHER WORKS OF FICTION

The reading of any novel is always enhanced by a knowledge of the author's body of work, their *oeuvre*; this helps to place the novel in context, while it also offers a better understanding of the author's chosen themes and narrative techniques. In the case of Proulx, who started late in life and then produced five books in rapid succession, it is especially interesting to trace the development of her writing and then seek to understand the place that *The Shipping News* occupies in that continuum. Over the next few pages, Proulx's other works of fiction will be discussed briefly. No previous knowledge of the texts is assumed (and therefore not too many details of the plot given away), since the purpose of this section is mainly to clarify the position that *The Shiping News* occupies in the body of the author's work.

Heart Songs, 1988

Heart Songs, the collection of stories published in 1988, contains many of the themes and techniques that would later become Proulx's trademark. Each story offers a glimpse into the life of people in the rural community of Chopping County. On the surface, nothing much happens as the people go about hunting deer and grouse, or fishing for trout. But beneath this surface of uneventfulness, Proulx hints at complicated stories to do with family relations, bad blood, and half-forgotten secrets. As with most of Proulx's fiction, these stories appear to have a timeless quality to them; were it not for the mention of trucks or electrical appliances, it would at times be very hard to determine when the action is supposed to be taking place. This technique is also used in *The Shipping News*, where Newfoundland is transformed into an almost mythical, magical place, an enchanted island perhaps, where late twentieth-century reality intrudes only briefly, often in the form of news that Partridge in LA relates to Quoyle. When the modern world intrudes into Chopping County, it does so via junk-mail coming through the post, as in the story "In the Pit", where "Papers, magazines, letters, bills, offers to develop her film in twenty-four hours or insure her credit cards against loss, fliers and folders" (p. 103) provide the connection between consumerist society and the quiet lives in rural communities. Above all, however, it is city people who come to the country for the weekend, or during the summer, who best represent the clash between the old and the new, the urban and the rural, and it is clear whose side Proulx is on. In "On the Antler", an unsavory character gets a new lease of life when visitors and summer residents arrive and decide that his less appealing features make him a "character": "They liked his stories, they read morals into his rambling lies and encouraged him by standing around the feed store playing farmer. [. . .] In late life he found himself admired and popular for the first time, and he was grateful" (p. 7). To satisfy the urban visitors' hunger and curiosity for "authentic" country life, little by little he sells off his family's possessions, so that "all his family's interests and enterprises were tangled together on the shelves as if he had drawn a rake through their lives and piled the debris in the store" (p. 8). This passage reminds us that, since any genuine connection with the land is becoming almost obsolete, rural life itself becomes a consumer event, or a product to be sold and bought not for any intrinsic value, but because of the lifestyle it is supposed to represent.

In "Heart Songs" the protagonist, Snipe, leaves his wife, his business and city life behind in order to pursue his interest in authentic country music. He finds a family who get together once a week to play music, and thinks he has struck gold: "These were real backwoods rednecks and he was playing with them. They were as down and dirty as you could get, he thought" (p. 77). Poverty and deprivation are romanticized by the people who have no understanding of the real hardship that a "simple" rural life entails. This is reinforced in the story when we learn that Snipe's new partner had taken a course in Peruvian weaving, hoping to sell her handiwork to Bloomingdale's: "You know they wanted indigenous Peruvian", she explains; "I couldn't help it if I didn't live in a filthy hut on top of the Andes, could I? They didn't want Vermont Peruvian" (p. 79). As the story draws to its conclusion, Snipe, by now disillusioned with his "rednecks", feels an overwhelming desire to listen to music by Haydn: "Haydn seemed safe and alluring like a freshly made bed with plump white pillows and a silken comforter. He could sink into Haydn" (p. 85). With Haydn's music, Snipe can opt out of the rural idyll that failed to live up to his expectations, and return to his own familiar cultural milieu.

In "The Unclouded Day", another outsider, Earl, wants local man Santee to teach him to shoot birds. Santee soon realizes that Earl has "the reflexes of a snowman". The city man's ineptness is reminiscent of Quoyle's various failed attempts to use a boat and adopt the lifestyle of his new, unfamiliar home in *The Shipping News*, but because he lacks Earl's pretensions he receives a much kinder treatment as a character. "Stone City" is one of very few stories that Proulx has written in the first person voice. Significantly, the narrator is an outsider who cannot comprehend the complexities of the life he has adopted. As in *The Shipping News*, family secrets and hidden traumas emerge only gradually, so that the truth is revealed to the narrator in fragments, which he has to piece together. In that respect, the outsider may also be seen as an image of the reader, to whom Proulx assigns a great responsibility. Because these stories, as well as Proulx's novels, do not rely on a strong plot, the reader has to be on her guard at all times, since what appears to be a descriptive passage, for example, may turn out to be the key to a mystery that unfolds as the story progresses. At the same time, the reader cannot know which of the story's elements will turn out to be clues, nor is it certain that all mysteries will be solved by the end. As we shall see again in relation to *The Shipping News*, this is what makes Proulx's fiction so challenging and demanding and, of course, so rewarding as well.

In *Heart Songs* Proulx also introduces a technique that she has used to great effect in most of her writing. She very often presents the readers with the effect long before she reveals the cause, so that various elements in each story appear inexplicable until the moment of revelation. A similar technique was used to great effect by Joseph Conrad in *Heart of Darkness*, and following Conrad scholar Ian Watt. I will be referring to it as "delayed decoding". Delayed decoding is a realistic narrative device to the extent that it mirrors the way in which we may be aware of things whose causes we have yet to discover. As such, it creates both suspense and a sense of bewilderment when used in narrative. At the same time, however, it is also an indication of the fact that the author has control over her creation, and chooses to manipulate her material in such a way as to suggest that characters' lives are unfolding in front of our eyes, when the truth is that their fate had been decided before the author began to write. Delayed decoding may assert the author's power, but as we shall see in the next chapter, it also allows the reader to interpret the text more freely.

Postcards, 1992

Of the three novels that Proulx has written so far, *Postcards* and *The Shipping News* are the ones that are often discussed in tandem because of certain similarities, whereas *Accordion Crimes* is seen as a different kind of fictional venture. *Postcards* tells the story of a farming family, the Bloods. Loyal Blood, the eldest son, kills his partner, Billy, for reasons which are only gradually, and even then imperfectly, revealed to the reader. He buries her corpse on the farm, and pretends that he is going away with her to build a new life. The story then traces his journeys across America, as well as the fate of the family he left behind. In his absence, his family is visited by tragedy and the farm eventually sold, but the irony is that although he regularly sends postcards home (which, along with cards sent by other characters, preface each chapter in the novel), he never gives an address, so that he doesn't know of his father's tragedy, nor that his crime was never really discovered (a man who finds the skeleton thinks it must be a peasant woman who died a very long time ago, and decides not to disturb her final place of rest). Despite its main focus being on one family, the novel has been read as an ambitious portrait of post-war America; the *New York Times* reviewer summed up the book's importance when he noted that "Story makes this novel compelling; technique makes it beautiful. What makes *Postcards* significant is that Ms. Proulx uses both story and technique to make real the history of post-World War II America". The combination of story and technique in the creation of a believable world is, of course, one of the main strengths of *The Shipping News* as well.

The *New York Times* reviewer compared the novel to *Native Son* by Richard Wright and *An American Tragedy* by Theodore Dreiser, while noting that Loyal Blood's travels across America are reminiscent of *Huckleberry Finn* without the laughter, and *The Grapes of*

Wrath without the hope. It is significant that all the writers Proulx is here compared to are men, and that the earliest of the books mentioned above was published in 1884, the most recent in 1940. As in *The Shipping News*, women in *Postcards* are given supporting roles, while the protagonist is an entirely believable male, and even though both novels are narrated in the third person, they both offer realistic insights into the inner lives of the male characters. As for the comparisons with much earlier books, these raise important questions which may be used in the study of literature more generally: what makes a novel contemporary? Is the time in which a novel is set more important than the time when it was written? And is the reviewer suggesting that Proulx's fiction is out of step with her time? This last question, at least, is easy to answer in the negative. The parallels with earlier novels emphasize a perceived continuity in American writing, and suggest that Proulx's novels are as appropriate for their age as those earlier books were for the age that produced and received them.

The time-span in *Postcards* ranges from 1944 to the 1980s, with important parts of the story unfolding against the backdrop of World War II, but this important historical event and the changes that followed it are only discernible through distant echoes in the text: a bomber crashes on a mountain, and Loyal Blood travels across America prospecting for uranium after the war. The effect that this achieves is to suggest that the characters depicted in the novel are affected by large-scale historical events, but personal circumstances, family relations and the bond with the land are the factors that are seen to provide the motivation for each character's behavior, while at the same time the text shows how larger, external events also help to shape the microcosm they live in. Dub, for example, makes money by leaving the farm and going into real estate in Florida. His change of fortune is propelled by his father's suicide and the selling-off of the farm, but it is also placed firmly within the context of

America's economic prosperity and growth after the war. Similarly, Jewell has to learn to fend for herself after her husband's death, but her steps towards independence also mirror the women's liberation movement. Jewell learns to drive and experiences feelings of exhilaration at the freedom driving gives her. She gets a job in a cannery, and she also starts selling hand-knitted hats and stockings to a ski shop. In a changing world, what was once a necessity (the woman knitting in order to keep her family warm), now becomes a luxury for the leisure market, and this is a reminder that Jewell's new-found freedom is not only indicative of new roles being available to more women, but also of the gradual disappearance of an older way of life. Her neighbor, Ronnie Nipple, advises her to sell the farm:

Well, Jewell, you got to know the market. Mink didn't even know there was a market, a real estate market. You folks kept to yourselfs up here. Missed out on a few things. Changes. It's not just what a farm'll bring for a farm, now. There's people with good money want to have a summer place. The view. That's important. See the hills, some water. (p. 128)

Passages such as this one are indicative of Proulx's critique of consumerism and commercialisation, and a lot of her fiction traces the effects of new economic and social trends on communities whose livelihood becomes threatened. Proulx herself points out that some months after *The Shipping News* was completed, the Canadian government imposed a fishing ban on Newfoundland, thus destroying not only people's livelihoods but also a traditional, centuries-old way of life.

What is remarkable about both *Postcards* and *The Shipping News* is that Proulx succeeds in being elegiac without being sentimental. Loyal Blood is never romanticized in *Postcards*, as can be illustrated by a passage early in the book where he remembers the farm he will never return to:

A sense of his place, his home, flooded him. [. . .] His blood, urine, feces and semen, the tears, strands of hair, vomit, flakes of skin, his infant and childhood teeth, the clippings of finger and toe nails, all the effluvia of his body were in that soil, part of that place. (p. 85)

The sense of loss and regret, and the farmer's strong connection with the land, are conveyed in a manner which is devoid of sentimentality, while the passage itself occurs immediately after Loyal's reminiscing about the woman he has killed, thus ensuring that the reader does not forget who this man is. As we shall see in the next chapter, the Newfoundland community in which Quoyle attempts to rebuild his life is also portrayed in a similar manner, emphasizing the strong link between man and nature, but never flinching from the cold, hard, unforgiving nature of the land.

As with all of Proulx's writing, language plays an important role in *Postcards*. The protagonist's name, Loyal, suggests that language may obscure and deceive, while at the other end of the spectrum language is seen to convey accurate, if often overlooked information about the world: when Loyal becomes a uranium prospector, he looks at maps and searches for places with names such as "Poison Spring" and "Badwater Canyon" (p. 171). He knows that these names actually describe the properties of these places in that they have been named for their deposits of selenium or arsenic, and he knows that where these elements exist uranium is also likely to be found. Language also provides some of the humorous passages in the book, usually in the form of stories that Jewell tells her daughter Mernelle. To relieve the tension when they're out looking for a lost baby, Mernelle asks her mother to repeat the story of how her grandfather used to count sheep:

Oh, that old thing, that was his way of counting sheep, the old, old style of counting. [. . .] See if I can remember it. Yan. Tyan. Tethera. Methera.

Pimp. Sethera. Lethera. Hovera. Dovera. Dick. Yan-a-dick. Tyan-a-dick. Tethera-dick. Methera-dick. Bumfit. Yan-a-bumfit. Tyan-a-bumfit. Tethera-bumfit. Methera-bumfit. Giggot. There! That's as much as I ever knew. Up to twenty. "Bumfit!" said Mernelle. "Bumfit." She started to laugh, as she always did. "Oh, bumfit!" She screamed with laughter. (p. 73)

From the literal, to the ironic, to the absurd, language is always used masterfully in all of Proulx's fiction.

Accordion Crimes, 1996

Accordion Crimes was the novel that followed *The Shipping News* to great acclaim. Critics had expressed worries that the spectacular success of *The Shipping News* would be hard to live up to, but *Accordion Crimes* confirmed Proulx's status as one of the best American writers of her generation. In some ways, *Accordion Crimes* combines Proulx's interest in both the novel and the short story form. It is a novel in the sense that it is a long narrative held together through its thematic unity, but at the same time it resembles a collection of stories in that it is made up of eight separate sections, each introducing new characters, but each also telling more than one story. What unites these fragments is the novel's protagonist, a green two-row button accordion. The novel begins in the nineteenth century with the unnamed accordion maker from Sicily, who travels to America in search of a better future for himself and his son. Following his horrific death by lynching, the accordion survives for another century, travelling across America as it falls into the hands of various immigrants for whom music serves as a reminder of their cultural past and as a means of survival in the new world.

Accordion Crimes differs from the two previous novels in several ways. It is much longer than its predecessors, it covers a significantly larger time-span, and it contains a much bigger cast of characters. This novel is also Proulx's most overtly political book. As we shall see in the next chapter, *The Shipping News* offers a subtle critique of contemporary American life, but it does so in ways which are mostly implicit. Both books undermine the dominant American narrative (or myth) of starting over, of creating a new, better life in a new home. In *The Shipping News*, Quoyle has to come to terms with his family history by revisiting his ancestral home; in *Accordion Crimes*, the various characters who inhabit the book learn that emigrating to America does not take them to the Promised Land of their imagination. Their lives are blighted by poverty, discrimination, hard, unrewarding work, and nostalgia for the places they have left behind. In its emphasis on the lives of the poor, *Accordion Crimes* is reminiscent of *Postcards*, but it is an even darker book dominated by violence and death, even though it is also relieved by moments of great humor.

Critics have remarked that, despite the fact that both *Postcards* and *The Shipping News* have a relatively small cast of characters and tell stories of ordinary lives, the two novels have epic resonances. This is certainly true of *Accordion Crimes*, which tells not only the stories of certain groups of immigrants but also, implicitly, much of the story of America and its people. The characters introduced in each of the book's eight sections are brought to life vividly, and their lives are documented in detail. Given their backgrounds in places as diverse as Sicily, Germany, Poland or Mexico, Proulx's meticulous research, and her ability to create fictional worlds out of her research material, are once again evident here. As in the previous novels, the stories she tells are of ordinary, seemingly unremarkable people, but, taken together, their stories create a larger picture dealing with some of the major issues in American society: race and racism, the politics of immigration, rural poverty, cultural identity, and the ways in which the larger forces of history affect individual lives. The entire novel is suffused with anger, violence and death, thus indicating Proulx's scathing critique of the foundations of American society.

In terms of technique, Proulx once again relies on her trademark delayed decoding to create mystery and suspense. When the hoped-for revelation finally comes, it is usually brutal and shocking, a fact which unsettles the reader. By undermining the pleasure of reading for the plot, Proulx indicates that the role of fiction is not always to provide comfort through the ordering of narrative, and that the anticipated happy ending is a fictional convention less likely to be found in real life. At the end of the fourth section, one character tells another of the protagonist's suicide, and the narrative concludes with the words: "Please, please, Emil," she thought, "don't ask how" (p. 276). The story of the suicide is then taken up in the following section almost twenty pages later, where we learn that the man cut off his own head. Given that this was a man who, after years of hardship and suffering, had found relative happiness, the readers had been led to suppose that his suicide may have been in a way an expression of that happiness: putting an end to his life when he was happiest. But even that small consolation is taken away when we finally discover the gruesome truth of his bloody suicide.

Proulx also employs another unusual narrative technique, which complicates the stories she tells and invites us to read the narrative in new, often conflicting ways. The novel is narrated in the third person by a narrator who remains mainly unobtrusive; we immerse ourselves into the stories that the narrator tells, and often forget that they are being related by an outside, unseen agent. Every now and then, however, the story is either interrupted or concludes with a few lines, or even a paragraph or more, which appear in parentheses and tell us what happened to characters "backstage", as it were. Through these parenthetical fragments, we are given information about some of the minor characters who drift in and out of the story, while other parenthetical sections tell of the characters' descendants and what happened to them years after the conclusion of the main narrative. As early as page 22, for instance, the accordion maker's brother sends letters from America describing his "handsome clothes, his position, his fine new bathtub (the bathtub in which he was fatally attacked a few years later by a Bohemian, lunatic with rage because Alessandro had kicked his son for making a noise on the stair; even then the old parents denied that their family was cursed)." In terms of the novel's thematic concerns, these parentheses emphasize the notion of fate and doom as much as that of progress and fulfilment. By allowing us a glimpse of both the sadness and the happiness in the lives of the characters and their descendants, Proulx has the opportunity both to suggest that to some extent fate determines human life, and also to show that, occasionally, vindication does occur through determination, progress and prosperity.

If we examine these passages in terms of technique, however, we come across a problem that will be addressed again when we look at *The Shipping News* in the next chapter. By telling us what happened to characters who, strictly speaking, are not part of the narrative, Proulx enhances the impression of realism: she is inviting us to believe that her fictional characters are "real" people who had children and grandchildren who do not exist in the book we are reading, and yet are no less real for that. At the same time, this technique of filling in life-stories undermines the impression of realism because it draws attention to the author's power over her characters, while it also draws attention to the fact that everything we read is filtered through a narrator who may reveal or withhold information as they see fit. In Chapter 2, we shall see how *The Shipping News* also invites its readers both to immerse themselves in the fictional world and to take a step back from it and remember that it is an artefact, a re-creation of lived experience.

Close Range: Wyoming Stories, 1999

In interviews she gave after the publication of *Accordion Crimes*, Proulx indicated that she has plans for several new novels. Before completing any of those, however, she published a collection of stories set in her new home of Wyoming. She thanked her publisher for allowing her "this side trip", adding that for her stories are very difficult to write, but that the idea of a collection of tales set in Wyoming "seized" her entirely. The book's epigraph comprises a quotation from a retired rancher, and it reads: "Reality's never been of much use out here", thus setting the tone for a collection of stories which, despite being mainly realistic, are often colored by hints of fantasy, fairy tale and myth.

In writing about the American West, Proulx inserts herself into a literary tradition that encompasses both realist writing and myth making. In "The Bunchgrass Edge of the World", an otherwise realistic story is disrupted by a tractor which speaks amorous words to the farmer's young daughter. Given that the farmer himself is called Aladdin, we are asked not to dimiss the speaking tractor as a figment of the girl's imagination, accepting it instead as a fact which does not violate the narrative's logic. The intermingling of fact and fiction is given a far more serious twist in "People in Hell Just Want a Drink of Water", where a man badly injured in an accident returns to his parents' farm and is castrated for exposing himself to the neighbors. He dies of gangrene, and the story concludes: "We are in a new millennium and such desperate things no longer happen. If you believe that you'll believe anything" (p. 128). In "55 Miles to the Gas Pump", a modern-day Bluebeard keeps the bodies of the women he has murdered in the attic of his house, where they are eventually discovered by his wife. The story suggests that isolation, boredom, and crime are the realities hidden beneath the myth of the pioneer who boldly leaves society behind in order to inhabit and tame the wilderness: "When you live a long way out you make your own fun" (p. 280), concludes the narrator with irony. Throughout *Close Range*, Proulx achieves a de-mythologizing of the West through the interweaving of fantasy and reality, and more specifically through the skillful way in which the fantasy elements somehow make the reality more real, and more frightening. "If there is any blood left in our romance with West, Annie Proulx [. . .] wrings it dry in her powerful new collection" wrote *New York Times* reviewer Christopher Lehmann-Haupt.

One of the most striking things about *Close Range* is the effect of effortlessness it conveys. Proulx is so successful in bringing to life the characters she creates that it is easy to forget that these are paper characters, made up of words, and dreamed up by a female author with an academic background. Her use of dialogue is a major contributor to this effect: even though phonetic transcriptions of regional accents are only used sparingly, they add a hint of local color which is enough to allow the readers to hear the voices of "real" people. In "The Mud Below", a bull rider returns home to his mother and little brother. When his brother tells him that he wants to get a buckle just like his, the rodeo rider says: "This ain't a terrific buckle. I hope you get a good one", but it is only when his brother replies "I'm going to tell Momma you said 'ain't' " (p. 61) that we are startled by this reminder of the importance of language in the construction of character.

Gender also plays a prominent role in these stories. Even though the main characters are, as usual, male, female characters are as fully realized as their male counterparts, and their plight highlighted in a way not often found in writings about the West. Proulx's stories tell of rape, sexual oppression, and the lonliess and hard work that are the harsh reality for many women. However, the most interesting story in terms of gender is "Brokeback Mountain", which tells a tale of male homosexual love and passion. The two men marry women and have children in an attempt to conform and be seen to lead "normal" lives, but their passion for each other does not diminish. Their community, however, does not tolerate any deviation from gender roles, and one of them, Jack, is killed in a homophobic attack. Near the story's conclusion, the surviving partner, Ennis, visits his dead lover's childhood home, and discovers that Jack has kept one of Ennis's old shirt hidden inside one of his own work shirts. This moving, tender moment both vindicates Proulx's comment about the superficiality of gender differences, and reminds us of the beauty and the poetic power that goes hand in hand with the harshness in all of Proulx's writing. Christopher Lehmann-Haupt could have been speaking of Proulx's entire *oeuvre* when he wrote of *Close Range*:

Why should you read these stories, then, if their characters' lives are so mean and their fates so inevitable? You read them for their absolute authenticity, the sense they convey that you are beyond fact or fiction in a world that could not be any other way. And you read them for their language, not lyrical but a wry poetry of loneliness and pain.

· **2**

The Novel

THE STORY

Here is an account of a few years in the life of Quoyle, born in Brooklyn and raised in a shuffle of dreary upstate towns.

Hive-spangled, gut roaring with gas and cramp, he survived childhood; at the state university, hand clapped over his chin, he camouflaged torment with smiles and silence. Stumbled through his twenties and into his thirties learning to separate his feelings from his life, counting on nothing. He ate prodigiously, liked a ham knuckle, buttered spuds.

His jobs: distributor of vending machine candy, all-night clerk in a convenience store, a third-rate newspaperman. At thirty-six, bereft, brimming with grief and thwarted love, Quoyle steered away to Newfoundland, the rock that had generated his ancestors, a place he had never been nor thought to go.

A watery place. And Quoyle feared water, could not swim. (p. 1)

Novels are best appreciated when read for a second time, and with the benefit of hindsight it is easy to see how this impressive opening of *The Shipping News* establishes some of the major themes and techniques that Proulx employs in the subsequent narrative of Quoyle's life in Newfoundland. In terms of technique, it becomes clear from these first paragraphs that this is not going to be a story narrated in a conventional manner. By condensing the rich panorama of a man's life up to the age of thirty-six into just over a hundred words, and announcing events that will unfold in subsequent chapters, the author signals that the story will not be narrated in a strictly linear manner. She also indicates that the story will be incomplete in ways that the reader is not expected to understand from the start. The haste with which the first thirty-six years of Quoyle's life are dispensed with indicates that our protagonist is not going to be a hero, but rather an anti-hero; not only a slightly grotesque figure, but also already a failure before the narrative proper begins. This is also emphasized by extra-diegetic elements, that is information which is not relayed by the novel's narrator and is therefore not part of the narrative itself. This first chapter is called "Quoyle"; it is quite common for a narrative to begin by introducing the protagonist, and therefore the title announces that Quoyle is going to be the hero of the novel. The first epigraph simply states that a Quoyle is a coil of rope, and while this may appear to be no more than a piece of factual information at best aimed at instructing the readers on how to pronounce the character's name, with retrospection we can see how rope will turn out to be a repeated symbol, or *leitmotif*, in the novel, as well as being an indication of Quoyle's own tangled life, and the complexities of the plot that the reader will be asked to unravel. The second epigraph, taken from *The Ashley Book of Knots*, like most epigraphs in subsequent chapters, further informs the reader that "A Flemish flake is a spiral coil of one layer only. It is made on deck, so that it may walked on if necessary." This is deliciously ironic, since Quoyle will indeed be walked on for a large part of the novel, until he begins to take charge of his own life and face up to his demons. Novels are endlessly re-written by readers, so that critics often point out that it is the reader who constructs the novel through the act of interpretation. However, at the same time novels also construct their readers, by instructing them in indirect and subtle ways on how to read and interpret. In this case, we are told to pay attention to the epigraphs and chapter titles, since they will be providing us with crucial information. However, this is not a simple as it seems at first. Neither the titles nor the epigraphs are always as transparent as this first one, so that the author may be understood to be "teasing" the reader by complicating the interpretative process as the book unfolds. This, in turn, mirrors the book's thematic preoccupations by highlighting the fact that meaning and signification are not readily available in either life or fiction.

The narrative begins with the close of the first phase in the protagonist's life; in doing so, it suggests that this will be a story of loss and endings as well as one of new beginnings. By page 20, Quoyle has lost both his parents, and has been insulted and dismissed by his brother, and that section of Chapter 3 concludes with these words: "By the time the aunt arrived, orphaned Quoyle was again recast by circumstance, this time as an abandoned and cuckolded husband, a widower" (p. 20). This sentence encompasses both loss and gain: the aunt's arrival will trigger the plot that will lead Quoyle to Newfoundland and to a partial recovery of his life and family ties, but by informing the reader that Quoyle will be cuckolded and end up a widower *before* narrating these events, the same sentence also helps to create a sense of doom by reminding the reader that everything has already happened, and that Quoyle is a victim of both the plot and of "circumstances" beyond his control.

Like most of Proulx's fiction, *The Shipping News* is narrated in the third person, with the narrator zooming in and out of the main characters' subjectivity. The phrase quoted earlier, "a place he had never been nor thought to go", establishes the narrator's authority over the character, and in this sense the formal aspect of the act of narration mirrors its thematic concerns in that it reflects the way in which Quoyle is manipulated by others. On the second page, the narrator goes on to add that Quoyle's "earliest sense of self was as a distant figure", thus suggesting that notions of identity and alienation will also be prominent in the subsequent narrative. The syncopated language employed from the beginning of the novel also creates a sense of alienation and detachment; personal pronouns are very often omitted, thus creating a distance between the internal world of the characters and the expression of their thoughts and feelings.

The *New York Times Book Review* described Proulx's first novel, *Postcards*, as "a meaty stew of archetypal plots and characters, their juices mingled in defiance of convention", and the same can be said of *The Shipping News*, where both plot and characters may be interpreted as symbols and archetypes. Quoyle is the archetypal (though unconventional) hero who embarks on a journey of self-discovery and re-invention which takes him to an island so far removed from the contemporary world he leaves behind as to appear almost mythical, or magical. The people who help him along the journey, first his aunt and then colleagues and friends in Newfoundland, can be read as mentors or guides who show him the way while also making him go through a series of dangerous rituals. When he first arrives at the *Gammy Bird* office, Quoyle is horrified to learn that his duties will involve covering car-crashes: "Car wrecks! Stunned with the probabilities of blood and dying people" (p. 69). He goes home and tells the aunt that he cannot do the job, because it will be a constant reminder of what happened to his wife. "Of course you can do the job", replies the aunt. "We face up to awful things because we can't go around them, or forget them. The sooner you get it over with, the sooner you say 'Yes, it happened, and there's nothing I can do about it,' the sooner you can get on with your own life. You've got children to bring up. So you've *got* to get over it. What we have to get over, somehow we do. Even the worst things." "Sure, get over it, thought Quoyle. Ten-cent philosophy" (p. 72). Quoyle dismisses the aunt's words because he doesn't know at this point in the narrative that she is speaking from personal experience. He does begin to "get over it" by the end of the book, but he does so by discovering his own strength, not simply by accepting advice, and part of that recovery also involves acknowledging that his misery neither is nor makes him unique. As the story unfolds, Quoyle and Nutbeem begin to suspect that Jack Buggit, the newspaper proprietor, may also be a magical agent. Nutbeem says: "what I don't know is if Jack understands what he's doing, if the pain is supposed to ease and dull through repetitive confrontation, or if it just persists, as fresh as on the day of the first personal event. I'd say it persists." Faced with his friend's pessimistic outlook, Quoyle surprises both himself and the reader by taking a more positive view: "It dulls it, the pain, I mean. It dulls it because you see your condition is not unique, that other people suffer as you suffer. There must be some kind of truth in the old saying, misery loves company. That it's easier to die if others around you are dying" (p. 221).

In addition to the "magical helpers" or mentors of the archetypal journey, Quoyle also has to contend with enemies who put him through tests. One such enemy is the setting of the novel itself, the unforgiving landscape and the harsh weather. In addition to having to fight with the elements in order to drive or restore the house, Quoyle, who fears water, has to buy a boat and use it every day. Reeder Grouch, a "sniggering" man, sells him a boat in which he nearly drowns, but he emerges from this ritual immersion stronger and more determined to get it right. The most interesting and menacing foe, though, is Quoyle's cousin Nolan. Cousin Nolan adds a touch of magical realism to the narrative, while being a seriously sinister figure who embodies some of the darker preoccupations of the novel. He ties knots and leaves them in Quoyle's house and car, hoping that they will bring misfortune, and when the house is destroyed in a storm, the cousin "trembled with pleasure at what he had conjured with wind-knots" (p. 318). More sinisterly, though, the cousin is Quoyle's dark "double". Where Quoyle cannot shake off the memory of his dead wife and form a new relationship, the cousin is rumored to have slept with his dead wife so that "no woman would have him again" (p. 162). Quoyle finally decides to visit his relative, and when the knock on the door is not answered he calls out: "Mr. Quoyle, Mr. Quoyle", and feels as if he were calling himself (p. 264). When the cousin finally comes to the door, Quoyle is forced to recognize the family resemblance: "The aunt's unruly hair; his father's lipless mouth; their common family eyes". Looking at his old, half-demented cousin, he sees an exaggerated version of himself: "Quoyle saw what he had sprung from. For the old man was mad, the gears of his mind stripped long ago to clashing discs edged with the stubs of broken cogs. Mad with loneliness or lovelessness, or from some genetic chemical jumble, or the flooding betrayal that all hermits suffer." Like an archetypal prophet or wizard, the old man picks up the knotted strings that Quoyle has brought with him and tosses them into the fire: "Them knots'll never undo now!" he says, and the reader understands that he is not just talking about the hex he has put on Quoyle, but about the family knots and ties that can never be undone, the past that cannot be altered.

From fairy tales to Homer's *Odyssey* to Bunyan's *Pilgrim's Progress* and beyond, the hero's journey, perilous or comical or both, is a powerful and instantly recognizable archetype. Moreover, *The Shipping News* partakes of a more specifically American tradition in which the journey represents re-invention and self-determination.

As the aunt tells Quoyle: "You've got a chance to start out all over again. A new place, new people, new sights. A clean slate. See, you can be anything you want with a fresh start. In a way, that's what I'm doing myself" (p. 27). It soon becomes clear, however, that these words are highly ironic, and that Proulx questions and parodies the narrative of a second, successful life in a new country. The opening pages of the novel have established a life that cannot be forgotten or left behind; there is little indication that geographical distance will help Quoyle put his traumas behind him, any more than Loyal Blood's running away from the farm and the scene of his crime helped him to build a new life in *Postcards*. Furthermore, it is ironic that the aunt says that going to Newfoundland will be a fresh start for her, too. Not only is it a return to her ancestral home but, more to the point, it is a return to the scene of childhood abuse and misery. Proulx is not reiterating the myth of American self-invention; rather, by employing those archetypal story elements, she exposes through subversion the falseness of the narrative of American self-invention, while also exposing the ways in which genre creates expectations for the reader.

Reading for the plot?

In 1973, French theorist Roland Barthes published his influential book *The Pleasure of the Text*. In it, he claimed that there are two systems of reading. The first one goes "straight to the articulations of the anecdote" and "ignores the play of language". In other words, this system of reading is based on the assumption that pleasure is derived from the plot, the story that a book tells. The second system, he added, "skips nothing; it weighs, it sticks to the text, it reads, so to speak, with application and transport". Barthes was not castigating those who read for the plot, and he certainly didn't privilege on system of reading over the other. He did, however, point out that the first system is more appropriate and best suited to the reading of nineteenth-century fiction, while the second is often the appropriate way of appreciating contemporary writing. To the relief of many readers who may have experienced secret feelings of guilt, he wrote: "Read slowly, read *all* of a novel by Zola, and the book will drop from your hands"; if the pleasure of the text comes mainly from the plot, it is legitimate to skip a few lines here and there so that the act of reading can keep up with the reader's narrative hunger. But "read fast, in snatches, some modern text", he added, "and it becomes opaque, inaccessible to your pleasure". *The Shipping News* makes great demands on the reader by being a text which requires both systems of reading to be applied. There are mysteries, hints and clues that produce the desire to accelerate the reading process, but solutions are often buried in the text and require "application" on the reader's part. This is a technique that Proulx had already used in *Postcards*. For instance, Jewell's death occurs in the second half of the penultimate sentence of chapter 38: "she felt only astonishment when the fatal aneurism halted her journey" (p. 242). Had the reader been distracted from those crucial eleven words, the next sentence, which concludes the chapter, would have offered no enlightenment: "Her hand clenched wild raspberry canes, relaxed".

The Shipping News is an elaborately constructed narrative whose complexities are only gradually revealed to the reader with repeated readings of the text. Proulx occasionally uses foreshadowing, the mentioning of events before the time when they occur in the sequence of the story; however, because the information is elliptical, the reader cannot know that a particular phrase or passage is a foreshadowing of events to come, and things fall into place slowly, as the narrative unfolds. By placing the reader in such an unprivileged position, Proulx is forcing them to re-enact Quoyle's own gropings, hesitations and false starts as he attempts to build a new life. When the four first arrive at the ancestral home, the aunt's reactions to seeing it after almost fifty years are described in the following manner: "The aunt was remembering a hundred things. I was born here, she said. Born in this house. Other rites had occurred here as well" (p. 43). The horrifying nature of those other rites will not be explicitly revealed for another two hundred and fifty pages or so (p. 297), by which time more clues will have been planted in the narrative. However, the above-quoted passage is not only interesting as an example of foreshadowing, but also in terms of the author's use of language in the creation of point of view. "The aunt was remembering things"; with the first sentence, the narrator, who is omniscient, offers us an insight into the aunt's mind. With the next sentence, the focus shifts from inside the aunt's mind to a report of her utterance: "I was born here, she said. Born in this house." And then something happens with the last sentence: we can no longer tell whether the narrator has returned to the aunt's internal consciousness, or whether the narrator is making a comment unrelated to the aunt's remark. In the context of books teaching us how to read them, this is a technique that Proulx uses on numerous occasions throughout the narrative, so that we soon learn to recognize that these sentences following a character's reported speech do relate to the person who had spoken last, filling in the things they left unsaid. However, even when the reader becomes accustomed to this through repetition, its effect remains vaguely unsettling: it suggests alienation and loneliness, indicating that each character stands alone, separate from the rest. But just as the novel's narrative brings the characters together, so the stories they tell one another within the book help to emphasise the connecting power of language and storytelling.

Some of the mysteries that the novel creates require a slowing down of the reading process instead of acceleration, which would not lead to the hoped-for answers. The book is structured in a very intricate, deceptively complex manner, and one of the effects that this structuring achieves is to force the readers to re-evaluate their interpretation as the story progresses. In this way, the novel itself reminds us that interpretation is conditional and subject to revision; that to interpret a text is not to have the final word on it. We are also reminded that life produces meaning in exactly this way, forcing us to re-evaluate and reconsider as we go along, and that therefore we should not expect fiction to be any easier to decipher simply because books are by necessity read in a linear manner from start to finish. Quoyle's eldest daughter, Bunny, is seen to have an over-active imagination. She thinks of lobsters as red spiders, and refuses to eat apricots because they look like "little fairies' bottoms". More seriously, she also appears to be developing a series of phobias and obsessions which force Quoyle to discuss the situation with his aunt. In this context, the first time Bunny is scared by a strange white dog with matted hair, the most obvious interpretation is to read the episode as occurring in her imagination only, perhaps an expression of the fears associated with a new, unfamiliar place in the mind of a recently orphaned child. Following this initial encounter, Bunny goes on to develop a fear of anything that might resemble the white dog, such as inanimate objects and indistinct shapes. When Quoyle and his aunt discuss this problem, she tries to rationalize: "Just think of what's happened. She's lost members of her family. Moved to a strange place. The old house. New people. [. . .] Things are upside down for her" (p. 132). With these words, the aunt is facilitating the interpretation which would explain Bunny's behavior as the result of trauma. Quoyle, however, insists that there's "something else", something "weird" about his daughter. This, in turn, offers the reader a second route to interpretation by introducing an element of the supernatural which does, in fact, run throughout the novel. These two ways of reading Bunny's behavior are perfectly valid for most of the novel, but when we finally come to page 264, two hundred and eighteen pages after

Bunny's initial encounter, we find out that the white dog is real after all: it belongs to Cousin Nolan, who has been trying to scare the family away, and therefore Bunny's fears were entirely justified.

Further instances in the novel help to clarify how the narrative offers itself to at least two interpretations. On page 100, there is a brief episode, contained within graphics of knots (of which more later), which shows the aunt alone in the house. She takes her brother's ashes to the outhouse, tips them down the hole, and then proceeds to urinate on them. "The thought that she, that his own son and grandchildren, would daily void their bodily wastes on his remains a thing only she would know". This episode offers another hint that will build up to the revelation Cousin Nolan makes near the end of the book, but without the benefit of hindsight the reader is authorized to read it in other ways as well. In addition to contributing to the depiction of the aunt as a lonely individual, willing to support others but somehow always remaining detached from them, the scene has the further function of increasing the sense that the setting of the story contains inexplicable mysteries, strange rites and enigmas.

Another example would be Billy Pretty father's saying about the different types of women. On page 115, Billy Pretty tells Quoyle that Wavey Prowse may be "the tall and quiet woman". "What does that mean?" asks Quoyle. "A thing me old dad used to say" is Billy's reply. Some sixty pages later, Billy finally explains that his father used to say that there are four women in every man's heart: the Maid in the Meadow, the Demon Lover, the Stouthearted Woman and the Tall and Quiet Woman. Quoyle fails to realize that this saying may have some bearing on his own life, but later on, when he thinks of his daughters as the Maids in the Meadow he finally understands who the other women are: Petal, the aunt and Wavey. Quoyle, like the reader, is an outsider, and just as he only gradually understands the import of other people's stories, and the extent of his relations to the world, so the narrative reveals itself to the reader in enigmatic fragments that have to be pieced together.

During a brief episode in chapter 23, Quoyle is awoken by strange noises in the house, in another scene which contributes to the mysterious atmosphere of the book (we later find out it was Cousin Nolan breaking in). Strange noises and flashes of light in the darkness, bizarre rituals and enigmatic sayings all help to paint a picture of Proulx's Newfoundland as an enchanted, magical place. This, to some extent, relies on and confirms the reader's expectations, since for the most part we are not expected to be familiar with the environment that serves as the book's setting. All the mysteries are eventually solved, but the way in which they are revealed to the reader through the book's structure facilitates the creation of two ways of reading which complement rather than contradict one another. When we don't know what the truth is, we accept and learn to enjoy the atmosphere of magic and the strange, weird goings-on that make up the plot. When we find out the truth, everything turns out to have a rational explanation, and we come to a better understanding of the novel's characters.

Another technical device which affects the reading and interpretation of the novel is the use of epigraphs at the beginning of each chapter. As mentioned earlier, some of these epigraphs can be read as "keys" to the chapter that follows. Chapter 33, for instance, mentions "magic nets, snares, and knots", and this is the chapter in which Quoyle finds out that Nolan has been practicing magic with his knots. Other epigraphs, however, are less easy to understand. Chapter 13, "The Dutch Cringle", begins by explaining that "A cringle will make an excellent emergency handle for a suitcase". The chapter is the one in which Quoyle meets the Melvilles on Hitler's yacht, so that the suitcase reference appears irrelevant. Eight chapters later, however, Quoyle finds a suitcase which turns out to contain Mr. Melville's head, so that it becomes clear that the earlier reference to suitcases was a hint of things to come, and just as Quoyle could never have anticipated that Mrs. Melville would kill and then behead and dismember her husband's body (which is also found by Quoyle later on), the reader too could not have anticipated the turn in the narrative.

Of all the structural techniques and devices that help both to complicate and to illuminate the novel's themes, knots and the various uses they are put to are the most prominent and complex ones. We have already seen some of the uses of the epigraphs from *The Ashley Book of Knots*, but their function does not end there. Knots are used throughout the book as symbols, and one of the things they stand for is family ties. Louise Flavin points out that Chapter 1 introduces Quoyle as a piece of rope without a knot: a man without connections. In addition, he is coiled around himself, indicating that he is self-absorbed and not interested in, or perhaps not capable of, forming relations. In this sense, the symbolism of the knots is a positive one in that it represents the extended ties between family members and communities. Looked at another way, however, Quoyle's early life is dominated by knots and ties. He remains greatly attached to the memory of his cruel, unfaithful wife, and is depicted as a loving, overprotective father from the start: "Quoyle loved, first Bunny, then Sunshine, loved them with a kind of fear that if they made it into the world they were with him on borrowed time, would one day run a wire into his brain through terrible event" (p. 23). In the early stages of the narrative, Quoyle is hopeless at his job, and the only friend he manages to make, Partridge, leaves for a new life in L.A. The children are the only ties Quoyle lives for, but the subsequent narrative shows how he learns to widen the extent of his relations. When he goes to Nutbeem's farewell party, a party in which only men are invited, he feels the "knots of fatherhood loosened for the night" (p. 254). Here is a thirty-six year-old man who has only been to "two or three parties

in his adult life, and never to one where all the guests were men".
Much later that night, when he finally leaves, tired and drunk, he
forgets that he's staying with Dennis and Beety and checks into an
inn for the night. Symbolically, then, the party helps to loosen the
ties of fatherhood and remind Quoyle that he is a man as well as a
father, and this is one of the many steps he takes in order to go from
being a series of fragments (widower, father, orphan) to being a fully
rounded individual.

Knots also have the contradictory functions of uniting and dis-
rupting the narrative. Their extensive use as epigraphs does provide
a structural unity, but the smaller graphics of knots which break up
each chapter in smaller units serve to interrupt the narrative flow.
This, in turn, mirrors what is happening within the narrative itself.
Some chapters, though not many, are not broken up by knots and
provide an uninterrupted narrative episode. Most, however, are di-
vided into smaller units which relate different episodes united only
by the chapter title. These smaller narrative fragments range from a
single paragraph to a few pages in length, and their use may be
understood as an almost cinematic technique: they provide brief
scenes in the lives of the characters, but in the absence of a unifying
whole, it is up to the reader to synthesize them into a coherent
story. This technique is a reflection of the manner in which stories
themselves are related within the novel. For instance, the harbor
master, Diddy Shovel, begins to tell Quoyle the story of Jack Buggit
and his estrangement from his son Dennis. The episode is one of
the longest uninterrupted units, taking up just over six pages. However, before Mr Shovel has had the chance to finish his story, the
phone rings and he has to cut it short, leaving both Quoyle and
the reader in suspense. A knot signals the end of the episode,
and the narrative moves on to relate Quoyle's purchase of a boat.
The story of the Buggits is taken up in the following Chapter
Twelve pages later, this time by Nutbeem, who completes the story

"as he heard it". This disruption of storytelling within the novel is an image of the novel itself, and it serves to illuminate one of the book's main concerns, the idea of community achieved through communication.

Symbolically then Quoyle, the coiled piece of rope with no knots, learns both to uncoil himself and to extend the ties that bind him to his new community. This, in turn, is reflected in the language the author uses. Quoyle's thoughts are conveyed to the reader in the third person, in a style that often amounts to little more than a collection of words not always bound together by verbs, pronouns or prepositions. Quoyle himself, alienated and with no clear sense of identity, often translates his life into humorous newspaper-style headlines: "Stupid Man Does Wrong Thing Once More" (p. 89). The novel suggests that it is when the fragments of language come together to create a narrative, a *story*, that a man can find a sense of identity and purpose, a fact which is also demonstrated by Quoyle's main job at the *Gammy Bird*, which provides the novel's title. When Quoyle first starts work at the paper, all he has to do is provide a list of all the ships coming in and out of the harbor: a collection of data, but no narrative, no story, no subjectivity. Chapter 17 bears the novel's title, "The Shipping News". In it, Quoyle takes the initiative for the first time and, instead of providing his usual list of ship's names, writes a story about the *Tough Baby*, the yacht built for Hitler and brought to Killick-Claw by the Melvilles. "The words fell out as fast as he could type. He had a sense of writing well" (p. 142). He does write well: Jack Buggit calls him into his office to congratulate him, and to ask him to make these little stories a regular feature of the shipping news. For the first time, his boss also asks Quoyle to call him "Jack" and not "Mr. Buggit": the first story he tells helps him to get accepted by the community, and helps him to discover a sense of self-esteem: "Thirty-six years old and this was the first time anybody had ever said he'd done it right" (p. 144).

The importance of storytelling that this novel so clearly emphasizes raises a host of other questions, some of which will be addressed in the next section.

AUTHENTICITY, REALISM AND FICTION

An interesting way of thinking about literature lies in examining the relationship between reality and authenticity on the one hand, and realism and fictional representation on the other. When *The Shipping News* was first published, many readers assumed that Proulx had spent most of her life in Newfoundland, mainly because of the strong sense of place the novel succeeded in conveying. The picture of a place that a novelist paints cannot easily be broken down into its ingredients, but generally speaking factors such as descriptions of the landscape and the weather, use of local dialect and names particular to the region, and elements relating to the island's economy, from government and politics to staples in the Newfoundlander diet, all contributed to the overall effect and helped to create a fictional microcosm that seemed like an accurate representation of reality. As we saw in Chapter 1, however, it was mainly Proulx's meticulous research rather than first-hand experience which allowed her to create such a plausible, seemingly authentic fictional world.

A similar thing happened with Louis de Bernières's best-selling novel, *Captain Corelli's Mandolin*; when it was first published, the assumption was that the author had spent a large part of his life on a Greek island, and possibly knew many older people; such was the degree of authenticity that his novel created that it was logical to assume that he was very familiar not only with Greek life, but with Greek life on an island during World War II. When interviewers quizzed the author about his extraordinary insights into an almost vanished way of life, it was a shock to discover that de Bernières had only spent a fortnight on Cephallonia on a package tour. As the novel's popularity grew and translations into other languages became available, an extraordinary thing happened: in Italy, people came forth claiming to be the "real" Captain Corelli, while in Greece members of the resistance movement condemned the book for its inaccurate portrayal of history. What this reminds us is that the line which separates reality from fiction is not always as clear as we might at first assume, and that the author is therefore asked to take on a big responsibility, a burden of *trust*. Whether a writer does or does not write from first-hand experience should not necessarily matter; we may admire the author's imaginative or empathetic powers, but other, more pressing questions need to be addressed.

The most interesting issue arising from novels which paint an utterly believable picture of a place, time, or event that readers are not expected to be familiar with is the issue of trust. Even when a story is self-consciously artificial and goes out of its way to remind the reader that it is fictional, its basis on fact often remains undisputed; although we have no trouble appreciating that characters and events are fictional inventions, at some level and to some extent (which we are often called upon to negotiate), we expect the author not to distort the reality the novel is based upon. In the case of *The Shipping News*, it is safe to assume that depictions of the landscape and the weather are based on reality. However, things become more complicated when we consider the picture of a community in which incest and child abuse are rife, and the locals enjoy reading about them in their weekly paper. Proulx has certainly taken a number of steps to separate fact from fiction, but her insistence on that separation indirectly forces the reader to consider the problematic relation between the two. It is interesting to note that the first instance of such a separation is not only extra-diegetic, but can actually be found before the dedication, acknowledgements or title page; before the novel itself has actually started. It is customary for publishers to include a disclaimer on the copyright page stating that any similarity to persons or events is not intended, but this convention is taken to parodic extremes in this novel. The disclaimer reads as follows:

This is a work of fiction. No resemblance is intended to living or dead persons, extant or failed newspapers, real government departments, specific towns or villages, actual roads or highways. The skiffs, trawlers and yachts, the upholstery needle, the logans, thumbies, and plates of cod cheeks, the bakeapples and those who pick them, the fish traps, the cats and dogs, the houses and seabirds described here are all fancies. The Newfoundland in this book, though salted with grains of truth, is an island of invention.

It is easy to miss this disclaimer because of the place it occupies in the book, but reading it enhances our understanding of the novel and its mixture of reality and invention. The novel, in both its form and its content, questions realistic representation and investigates the role that language plays as mediator between lived experience and expression.

The Mockingburg Record and The Gammy Bird

In a recent BBC radio interview, Proulx said that for a long time she had wanted to write a book with a journalist as its main character, because that would give her the opportunity to explore culture and society. Quoyle's initial ineptness as a newspaper man, coupled with the humorous depictions of the quality of the two papers he works for, provide yet another angle through which to approach the novel and seek to understand the interaction between reality and fiction. The first paper for which Quoyle works is the *Mockingburg Record*, described by the managing editor as "a family paper. We run upbeat stories with a community slant". The narrator then proceeds to extend the editor's description by adding that the *Record* "specialized in fawning anecdotes of local business people, profiles of folksy characters; this thin stuff padded with puzzles and contests, syndicated columns, features and cartoons. There was a self-help quiz: — 'Are You a Breakfast Alcoholic?' " (p. 5). In other words, the *Record* is a newspaper with hardly any news in it. This gives the author an opportunity to poke fun at the proliferation of media, and the increasingly absurd lengths to which they will go in order to secure a readership and be seen to be providing a service to the community. The absence of "real" news from this paper leads us to question the distinction between reality and fiction; the "fawning anecdotes" and "folksy characters" of the *Mockingburg Record* might as well be fictional anecdotes and fictional characters.

Beneath the humor of the paper's depiction lies a question that has preoccupied American writing for a long time. It found its most articulate and memorable expression in 1961, when Philip Roth published an essay called "Writing American Fiction", in which he claimed that contemporary American life was beginning to elude comprehension and exceed the limits of the imagination. "The daily newspapers", he wrote, "fill us with wonder and awe (is it possible? is it happening?), also with sickness and despair." And Roth's conclusion was

Simply this: that the American writer in the middle of the twentieth century has his hands full in trying to understand, then describe, and then make *credible* much of American reality. It stupefies, it sickens, it infuriates, and finally it is even a kind of embarrassment to one's own meagre imagination. The actuality is continually outdoing our talents, and the culture tosses up figures almost daily that are the envy of any novelist.

Roth went on to assess the various writing strategies that novelists of his generation had employed in order to deal with this problem,

and he concluded that there was "a voluntary withdrawal of interest
by the fiction writer from some of the grander social and political
phenomena of our times." In J. D. Salinger he found "a spurning
of life as it is lived in the immediate world". In Bernard Malamud
he discerned no "specific interest in the anxieties and dilemmas
and corruptions of the contemporary American Jew"; Malamud's
novels, he claimed, where "timeless" and "placeless". In Saul Bellow and William Styron he saw a tendency to depict heroes who
are discontent, often disgusted by contemporary America. Their
response is to leave their country and seek fulfilment elsewhere and
this, according to Roth, represents a reluctance on the part of the
writer to address problems and seek to offer answers. The Bellow
novel he was referring to was *Henderson the Rain King* in which
the eponymous hero tells the story of his extended stay in Africa; an
Africa, Roth noted, with no nationalism or riots or apartheid. The
novel ends with Henderson flying back to New York. The plane
makes a refuelling stop in Newfoundland, and Henderson gets out
of the plane to celebrate the new self he has created for himself in
Africa. "The picture has stayed with me since I read the book a year
ago", wrote Roth, "of a man who finds energy and joy in an imagined Africa, and celebrates it on an unpeopled, icebound vastness
[in Newfoundland]". For Roth, depictions of "imagined" or "unpeopled" places meant that writers were turning their backs on contemporary reality, retreating into worlds created by the imagination.

In the years following the publication of Roth's essay, a new
literary movement appeared in America which dominated the 1960s
and early 1970s. Writers such as John Barth, William H. Gass,
Robert Coover and Donald Barthelme were associated with what
came to be known as "metafiction". As the term suggests, this was
fiction about fiction; it no longer pretended or attempted to represent reality in uncomplicated ways, and revelled instead in the
intricacies of constructing fictional worlds. As Malcolm Bradbury

noted, in this kind of writing narrative was "often concerned with the metaphysics of writing, the options of story, or the problems of language". A typical example would be John Barth's "Life Story", which is the story of a fictional character who is a writer writing a story about a writer who begins to suspect that he is not real but a fictional character in a story about a story about a man who thinks he is a fictional character . . . and so on, theoretically *ad infinitum*. Where Roth was advocating a dedication to reality as it is experienced by the author, these writers reminded us that fiction is only ever make-believe, the re-presentation of reality which, being filtered through language, narrative, plot or character, cannot and should not claim to be the thing it uses conventions to reflect. This challenge to realistic modes of representation was experimental in its nature, and to many readers it seemed intellectually stimulating and challenging, but not as rewarding as writing which at least sought to re-affirm some relation to reality. As Malcolm Bradbury noted, the "revolutionary spirit" that such writing represented began to fade in the 1970s, so that by the 1980s there was a more "peaceful intercourse" and a "profitable trade" between fiction that was concerned with its own construction and fiction which sought to affirm its relation to reality. *The Shipping News* is best understood as a novel which profits from this trade: it is "knowing" (though not explicit) about its own status as a fictional creation, but at the same time it borrows from the realist tradition.

The second paper that Quoyle works for, the *Gammy Bird*, is an eccentric and somewhat fantastical fictional invention, but beneath the exaggeration and the comic effect, it instructs us on how to read the novel; it indirectly tells us what issues to look for, and what to pay attention to. It serves as an image of the novel itself in various ways: in its blurring of fact and fiction, in the attention it draws on how language is not a transparent medium but a vehicle which distorts in the process of transition from real, lived life to representations of it, and in its mixture of the trivial and the serious. Nut-beem steals stories off the radio and rewrites them "in his plummy style", which "bloody misbegotten Card takes the liberty of recasting in his own insane tongue"(p. 58). This may be bad practice for a newspaper, but it is a useful reminder of how stories are transmitted as they are retold and inevitably revised. Every sentence in the paper is "so richly freighted with typographical errors that the original authors would not recognize their own stories", as Nutbeem complains, to which Tert Card replies that it does not matter because the stories are "stolen fiction in the first place" (p. 59). Stealing fiction and recasting it in different language is, in a sense, what all novels do. Since nothing exists in a vacuum, and novels are written and read in a specific context, "stealing" refers to the fact that the notion of originality necessarily recedes into a distance that seems forever out of the writer's, and the reader's, grasp. Meanwhile, the typos which distort the news printed in the *Gammy Bird* are useful reminders that any kind of storytelling relies on language as a vehicle of expression, and therefore the telling of the story is as important as, or even indistinguishable from, what it has to say.

The next question that is worth asking in the context of the novel's treatment of reality is whether it belongs to the tradition of American novels that Roth criticized for choosing the "easy" way of taking their protagonists away from a reality they do not approve of. Is Quoyle's relocation from New York to Newfoundland meant to represent an escape, and therefore a denial to engage with contemporary ills? And is the Newfoundland he goes to a rural idyll standing in opposition to urban corruption, or even an imaginary place whose function is to assist the hero's recovery? The novel does invite the reader to pose these questions, but the answer is no. The narrative begins by painting a picture of a disaffected man in a crumbling community. As early as page 10, Quoyle is shown to de dissatisfied with the quality of life in Mockingburg:

Quoyle, stuck in bedraggled Mockingburg. A place in its third death. Stumbled in two hundred years from forests and woodland tribes, to farms, to a working-class city of machine tool and tire factories. A long recession emptied the downtown, killed the malls. Factories for sale. Slum streets, youths with guns in their pockets, political word-rattle of some litany, sore mouths and broken ideas. (pp. 10–11)

This brief portrait of Mockingburg, tracing its decline from agriculture to industrialization and in so doing offering a brief but sharp critique of economic and social change, sets up the scene for Quoyle's escape. We are invited to assume that this will be the story of man who leaves this squalor behind and goes in search of a better environment in which to fulfil his potential. At the same time, Quoyle is seen to be an apolitical man, oblivious to the wider forces that shape life around him:

He abstracted his life from the times. He believed he was a newspaper reporter, yet read no paper except *The Mockingburg Record*, and so managed to ignore terrorism, climatological change, collapsing governments, chemical spills, plagues, recession and failing banks, floating debris, the disintegrating ozone layer. Volcanoes, earthquakes and hurricanes, religious frauds, defective vehicles and scientific charlatans, mass murderers and serial killers, tidal waves of cancer, AIDS, deforestation and exploding aircraft were as remote to him as braid catches, canions and rosette-embroidered garters. (p. 11)

Unlike its protagonist, though, the novel itself is not removed from reality. However, because the novel does not set out to be primarily or even explicitly political, the social critique it offers is subsumed into the more personal, intimate story it tells. We have already seen how Proulx's narrative technique allows her to paint a "double" picture of Newfoundland: a magical place of archetypal figures, a place where strange rituals take place, but also a "real" place in which all the strange goings-on are seen to have a logical explanation. A good example that illustrates how a similar technique is applied when it comes to political matters can be found in the "Gammy Bird" chapter, where Jack Buggit tells Quoyle how he came to be a newspaper proprietor. On one level, the story functions as an example of how Quoyle is gradually accepted into the new community by people telling him stories. On another level, this particular story shows how a man's personal life is affected by the greater forces of the society he lives in. Jack Buggit begins by recalling his early days as a fisherman. He remembers Newfoundland before confederation with Canada (decided by referendum in 1949, narrowly won by 51%) as a harsh, lawless place lured into the modern world by the promise of electricity, roads, telephone and radio. But the price to be paid for centralized government and modernization was the decline of the fishing industry which had shaped the lives of the islanders: "And the fishing's went down, down, down, forty years sliding away into nothing, the goddam Canada government giving fishing rights to every country on the face of the earth" (p. 65). The antithesis of Jack Buggit is Tert Card, who embraces change wholeheartedly, and dreams of retiring to Florida. The speech he makes on page 200 is a reminder not to romanticise or feel false nostalgia for the "good old days": "Nobody, nobody in their right mind would go back to them hard, hard times. People was only kind because life was so dirty you couldn't afford to have any enemies. It was all swim or sink. A situation that makes people very sweet."

From his position as an outsider, Quoyle listens to both points of view but subscribes to none, and the novel itself seeks to attain a similar position, avoiding simplistic polarities. As we have seen in the first chapter, Proulx's novels tend to impart a sense of timelessness which helps to emphasize and vivify the author's chosen themes. However, enough references are incorporated into all her

writing to enable the reader not only to work out a story's chronol-
ogy, but also to discern Proulx's subtle critique of the culture she
writes about. The Newfoundland that Quoyle comes to does not
strike the reader as a modern place. Apart from references to cars,
trucks, television and video, there is little to indicate that the action
takes place at the end of the twentieth century, an era dominated
by technological progress and consumerism. The novel seems to be
aware of that impression it creates, and once again uses Quoyle to
explore the readers" own pre-conceptions. The first time Quoyle
visits the harbormaster's office, he is shown logbooks consisting of
loose leaves which record each ship's arrival and departure. "Ha-
ha," said Quoyle. "I'd think they'd get you a computer. These
logbooks look like a lot of work" (p. 80). The harbormaster then
directs him to another part of the room, shows him his state-of-the-
art computer, and prints out the information that Quoyle needs.
"Now you'll remember that we do it two ways", says the harbomaster
and grins, and the reader feels as humiliated as Quoyle for assuming
that things would be done the old-fashioned way.

Following this early warning not to jump to the wrong conclu-
sions, the narrative continues to paint a picture of a rather old-
fashioned community, seemingly far removed from contemporary
ways of life. Then, on page 220, the modern world intrudes in the
form of a letter sent to Quoyle by his old friend Partridge, who has
moved to California. Partridge tells Quoyle all about his latest ac-
quisitions: a camcorder, the Ultima Chef's Gas Grill, a great sound
system with digital signal processing that could play video laser discs
and CDs at the same time in different rooms at different volumes.
Seventy pages later, however, the consumerist dream turns into
nightmare, as Partridge phones with news of the race riots in L.A.
"Not only L.A," he says. "It's like the whole country got infected
with some rage virus, going for their guns like it used to be you'd
look at your watch." "It hit me [. . .] what a fucking miserable

crazy place we're in" (pp. 290–1). Like Partridge's L.A, and by implication the USA more generally, mainland Canada also appears in the narrative in the form of distant echoes. Nutbeem is teased for wanting to include a story on Canada in his foreign news report: "There are some of us, Nutbeem, who do not think of Canada as a foreign power, said Card" (p. 245). The humor of this passage subtly draws attention to the fact that, even though the larger forces that shape individual lives are not always explicitly mentioned in the narrative, their presence should not be ignored. Similarly, Proulx's depiction of family ties and interpersonal relations encourages the reader to think not only of the microcosm the author has created, but also of the wider ideological issues which are implicit in such depictions.

THE FAMILY, RELATIONSHIPS AND GENDER

In his recent study of contemporary American fiction, Kenneth Millard has pointed out that the American family "is widely regarded as the sacred cornerstone of the American social project and it is perceived as fundamental to the happiness and success of the individual, the nation, and corporate life". By bringing this observation to bear on the study of American literature, Millard has concluded that "Since Nathaniel Hawthorne's *The Scarlet Letter* (1850) the family unit has been used to examine the particular conditions of the wider culture to which it belongs". In this sense, it useful to think of *The Shipping News* both in terms of its contribution to American ideas about the family, and in comparison with other works of contemporary fiction (Millard discusses *The Shipping News* along with novels by Toni Morrison, Russell Banks, Jay McInerney, Barbara Kingsolver and John Dufresne in a chapter called "Family Values").

In common with much contemporary American fiction, *The Shipping News* deals with an unconventional family model: two motherless children who think their mother has gone to sleep in New York, Quoyle the grief-stricken father, and the aunt who has never told her family that she is a lesbian, but who has been sexually abused by Quoyle's father, her own brother. The aunt is never seen to be maternal, and her relationship with Quoyle's daughters is under-represented in the novel. Wavey, whom Quoyle eventually marries, is not a conventional mother-figure either. She treats the little girls like diminutive adults when she first meets them, shaking their hands and saying "how do you do", and her relationship with her new stepdaughters is cemented by her explaining to Bunny, the eldest, that her mother is dead and will never come back to life. The sexual abuse stories that the *Gammy Bird* runs each week also paint a bleak picture of family life, since most of them involve incest. Proulx is eager to emphasize that this phenomenon is neither new nor more prevalent in Newfoundland than in other places; instead, the emphasis lies on the sad fact that it is happening at all, and the criticism is aimed at those who take pleasure in reading about it in the papers (p. 218). In representing family life as often dysfunctional, and a major contributor to trauma in adult life, Proulx is not only representing a reality that is being talked about more than ever before. She is also undermining the narrative which posits the traditional family as the very foundations of happiness and fulfilment, and ultimately she demonstrates the family's capacity for hurt as well as redemption.

We have already seen how Proulx uses Quoyle's relocation to Newfoundland to interrogate the mythical American journey of self-fulfilment, and it is important to note that, for Quoyle as much as for his aunt, going to Newfoundland in many ways represents a return rather than a fresh start. Quoyle's family ties have been severed before he undertakes his journey, but his new home will help him to realise the extent of his relations beyond the nuclear family. The first three chapters of the novel are called, significantly, "Quoyle", "Love Knot" and "Strangle Knot", and these are the only three to deal with Quoyle's life before Newfoundland. "Quoyle", as we have seen, introduces the protagonist to the readers. "Love Knot" is dedicated exclusively to Quoyle's relationship with Petal, unlike most other chapters which encompass more than one theme. "Strangle Knot", the third chapter, is much more ambiguous than the second one. This is the chapter that tells of Quoyle's parents' suicide, and it also shows how Quoyle is treated with contempt by his brother who does not even want to attend his parents' funeral. The same chapter introduces Agnis Hamm, and tells of Petal's flight and eventual death. The epigraph informs us that "The strangle knot will hold a coil well . . . It is first tied loosely and then worked snug". But which of the characters that this chapter deals with is the one holding Quoyle? His parents, his brother and his wife all "strangle" him in various ways, showing family ties to be destructive. Instead of the traditional suicide note, Quoyle's father phones the newspaper and leaves a message on the answering machine. He asks his son to get in touch with his brother and his aunt, and then goes on to say "I don't know where the rest of them are. They weren't—" (p. 19), and here the answering machine cuts him off, and in so doing cuts off Quoyle's own family history. But Agnis Hamm does get in touch with her nephew, and she is also "tied loosely and then worked snug" as her relationship with Quoyle develops. Hers, however, is a benevolent knot that will teach Quoyle the joys of family ties.

Quoyle begins a new life in Newfoundland unaware of the dark secrets and bad reputation of his ancestors. When Billy Pretty finally tells him that Cousin Nolan bears him and the aunt a grudge, Quoyle shudders to hear that the cousin is the "old style of Quoyle": "Jesus. [. . .] What do you mean, 'old style of Quoyle.' I don't know the stories" (p. 162). That last sentence says more than Quoyle might realize; he doesn't say "I don't know who my ancestors were", he says "I don't know the stories". This implies that family history is made up of stories, which are told and re-told, and passed down the generations; they often survive in the wider community and, in this instance, they make it harder for Quoyle to be the "author" of his own life story. The myth of the self-made man who makes a clean start is shown to be false, because family histories and family stories are always woven into an individual's life story. To their credit, however, the locals do not reject Quoyle because of his ancestors' notoriety. Billy Pretty tells him:

Omaloor Bay is called after Quoyles. Loonies. They was wild and inbred, half-wits and murderers. Half of them was low-minded. You should have heard Jack on the phone when he got your letter to come to the *Gammy Bird*. Called up all your references. [. . .] We was on pins and needles waiting to see what come in the door. Thought you was going to be a big, wild booger. (p. 162)

Both this dark legacy, and the fact that his new friends are willing to acknowledge it and still accept him into their community, are factors which help Quoyle to put his own life into perspective. The women in Quoyle's life function in a similar manner, embodying both a dark past and a promise of redemption.

We have already seen in the previous chapter how Proulx challenges conventional wisdom and misconceptions concerning women's writing, and *The Shipping News* is no exception. The novel's male protagonist is a fully realized character, but is the same true of the female characters in the book? Does the saying about the demon lover, the maid in the meadow, the stouthearted woman and the tall, quiet woman reinforce gender stereotypes, or does it serve as a warning against such stereotypes? There is no easy, unambiguous answer to this question, but a closer look at the aunt, Petal and Wavey may help to shed some light on this problem.

Petal is indeed depicted as the Demon lover. She treats Quoyle with contempt, and she has no maternal feelings whatsoever. She has a voracious sexual appetite, and she does not hesitate to bring her lovers into the house while Quoyle is asleep upstairs, and when she runs away she tries to sell her children to a pornographer. The aunt's verdict is that she is "a bitch in high heels" (p. 24). However, the one person whom Petal hurts most is not willing to demonize her. In Quoyle's view, Petal's behavior was simply a manifestation of her need to be loved: "Some people probably thought she was bad", he tells the aunt, "but I think she was starved for love" (p. 23). By asking us to accept Quoyle's faithfulness to the memory of such a person, the novel may be suggesting that Petal was, indeed, a more complicated character than the aunt gives her credit for. At this point, it might be worth keeping in mind that we expect fiction to make sense in a way that real life often doesn't. It could be that Quoyle's devotion to Petal does not make sense in *fictional* terms, whereas real life would provide ample illustrations of unhappy relationships and inexplicable attachments to people. This is a question that is worth pursuing further, as it applies to our expectations of fiction more generally.

The aunt is the stouthearted woman who brings stability and order to Quoyle's life. She is self-reliant, resourceful and decisive, and in many ways she challenges stereotypical depictions of femininity. Her name, Agnis Hamm, is only mentioned two or three times in the narrative; more often, she is simply "the aunt". This emphasizes the importance of family relations in the novel, and it reminds us that the aunt is in many ways an "agent" of the plot: she has a specific function relating to Quoyle's gradual recovery, and when Quoyle has grown sufficiently in confidence and inner strength, she disappears from the book. Kenneth Millard worries that the book may be suggesting that the aunt's sexual orientation is related to the sexual abuse she suffered in the hands of her brother; such a reading would imply that lesbianism is the "unnatural" result of an unnatural heterosexual union. Millard does not pursue this line of argument, and it is easy to see why. He is right to remind his readers of the need to examine a novel's political agenda, no matter how well hidden it may be, but this particular novel does very little to encourage such a reading. Far from enabling the reader to trace the development of the aunt's character back to her childhood trauma, the book celebrates her recovery and demonstrates how she has been able to put the past behind her in a way that is neither a denial or repression of that past, nor an unconvincing, implausible triumph of strength and forgiveness.

The aunt's unwillingness to reveal to Quoyle that Warren was a woman may be used as further evidence that the novel is providing an unsympathetic portrayal of a lesbian, suggesting perhaps that she is ashamed of or uncomfortable with her sexuality. Again, however, the context of the novel makes such a reading difficult to support. The aunt has fond memories of her partner, and thinks about her a lot. When she tells Quoyle about their relationship, we only notice the deliberate absence of pronouns that would identify Warren as female because we *know* she was female. The suggestion here is that gender is almost irrelevant, in the same way that the author's gender seems irrelevant to her creation of fictional characters: it is the strength and quality of the partnership between Agnis and Irene that matters, just as it is the story of Quoyle, and not his maleness, that makes the novel interesting.

Quoyle is on the whole a likeable character, but his behavior towards the aunt is not always commendable. It takes him a long time to ask her what she does for a living: "I'm embarrassed to say I don't know", he tells her. "I mean, I never thought to ask". The narrator adds: "Had blundered into the unlikely journey knowing

nothing, breathing grief like a sour gas. Hoping for oxygen soon"
(p. 49). Quoyle's grief causes him to be self-centerd, indifferent to
the people around him, but his relationship with the aunt does help
gradually to bring him out of his destructive introspection. At this
point in the narrative, she tells him that her work is "upholstery",
and Quoyle asks no further questions. Seventy-two pages later, he
finds out from the Melvilles that she is working in yacht upholstery,
and that she is very good at her job. " 'I swear until today I never
knew such a thing existed' ", he tells her. " 'I would have been less
surprised if you'd been a nuclear physicist'. It came to him he knew
nearly nothing of the aunt's life. And hadn't missed the knowledge"
(p. 123). The fact that he acknowledges his own lack of interest for
the first time indicates that Quoyle is beginning to uncoil, coming
out of his introspection. As the narrative progresses, and Quoyle
begins to rebuild his connections with the world around him while
also growing in confidence, the aunt's role diminishes in signifi-
cance. Quoyle finally reaches a point where he can begin to solve
his own problems and take control of the situation. When he out-
lines the various options for having the snow cleared from the road
leading to their house, the aunt is surprised: " 'You have been
thinking of all the angles,' said the aunt. Dryly. She was used to
being the one who figured things out" (p. 227). Quoyle, still oblivious to the fact that he may be hurting her feelings, goes on to
suggest that the family relocate for the winter. He is thinking of
staying with the girls in Nutbeem's trailer, and asks the aunt
whether she would have trouble finding somewhere to live since
there isn't enough room for all of them. It would appear, then, that
Quoyle has not yet reached the point where he can find a balance
between looking after himself and his daughters and solving his own
problems on the one hand, and acknowledging the emotional and
practical needs of other people on the other. When Cousin Nolan
finally reveals to him what had happened to the aunt he does finally

begin to empathize, but it is also Wavey Prowse who helps him in his transformation.

Proulx's tendency to create asexual or non-gendered characters continues with her depiction of Wavey Prowse. Wavey is often seen through Quoyle's eyes, but despite being the object of his affections (or at least his attention at first), she is never described in terms of sexual attractiveness, or feminine attributes. Their long, reluctant courtship is not shown to be based on physical attraction, and Proulx steers clear of the convention that requires a story's hero to end up with an attractive female, as a reward for the better qualities that lie beneath his grotesque appearance. Wavey's lack of overt sexuality serves as a contrast to the over-sexed Petal, and learning to love her is part of Quoyle's move toward maturity and integration into his community. In the section that follows we shall explore whether the union between Wavey and Quoyle makes the novel a love story, and whether the ending is as happy ending.

HAPPILY EVER AFTER? THE ROLE OF THE READER

Proulx has on repeated occasions claimed that she gave *The Shipping News* a "happy" ending in response to criticisms that her first novel was too bleak and wholly unrelieved by any kind of happiness. "*The Shipping News* was a writing exercise for me", she told Katharine Viner. "I was so tired of people saying *Postcards* was dark, and after I'd heard it for the 900th time I thought—OK, so a happy ending is wanted, isn't it. So I thought I'd have an amusing time writing a book with a happy ending. Although the happy part of *The Shipping News* was the absence of pain, so it's a sort of happiness by default". When she recently put that view to a group of readers for a discussion broadcast on BBC radio, a member of the audience said she was disappointed to hear that the happy ending was ironic, because she had taken it to be sincere. Proulx responded to this by remarking that a book, any book, is a collaboration between the author and the reader. "However you read it that's how it is", she told her disappointed reader. Other contemporary writers have written on the subject, and they all seem to agree that the reader plays a big role in constructing the meaning of a novel. However, this liberating approach creates a new problem: if the book means what the reader thinks it means, if there is no single "correct" interpretation of a book, can there be an "incorrect" way of reading a novel? Is the reader ever wrong?

Umberto Eco, best known to a wide audience as the author of *The Name of the Rose,* but also an eminent scholar, has attempted to answer this question by drawing on his own dual role as novelist and critic. *The Name of the Rose* is both a detective story and a complex philosophical investigation; as such, it creates as many questions as its narrative appears to answer, inviting the reader to take up the role of the detective. For years after the publication of the novel, Eco would receive letters from readers suggesting answers to the various questions that the book raised. He had to admit that some of the interpretations the readers suggested had never occurred to him; not while he was writing the book, nor afterwards. This, he claimed, did not make the readers" interpretations any less valid or significant. What the text says, Eco claimed, is not necessarily the same as what the author thought he or she was saying, and since the reader has access to the text but not to the author, if sufficient textual evidence can be provided, there is no reason why a reading of the book which the writer had not thought of should be considered in any way inferior. "There are cases", Eco wrote,

in which the author is still living, the critics have given their interpretations of his text, and it can then be interesting to ask the author how much and to what extent he, as an empirical person, was aware of the manifold interpretations his text supported. At this point the response of the author must not be used in order to validate the interpretations of his text, but to show the discrepancies between the author's intention and the intention of the text.

Eco's views are informed by an argument put forth by Roland Barthes in 1968, when he published the provocatively titled essay "The Death of the Author". Barthes argued that it was wrong to assume that authorship equals authority. "To give a text an Author is to impose a limit on that text, to furnish it with a final signified, to close the writing." As the capitalization of the word Author indicates, Barthes was speaking about the concept of the writer as a God-like figure whose mysterious ways the reader was called upon to decipher, or at least try to understand. Barthes argued that this model of the author was inappropriate for the study of literature, and that the task of the reader should not be to attempt to reconstruct or guess what the author meant to say. The act of reading should not be understood as a search for the writer's "authoritative" version of the text, because a text's unity lies "not in its origin but in its destination", that destination being the reader: "the birth of the reader must be at the cost of the death of the author", concluded Barthes.

Barthes's essay had a very large impact on literary studies, but it also created a new problem which has preoccupied many critics and theorists since. If we no longer believe that the author has the right to limit our interpretation of a text, does it then follow that anything goes, that any interpretation is correct as long as it is based on textual evidence? Umberto Eco took up this question, and suggested that a limit should be drawn at some point: "But certain interpretations can be recognized as unsuccessful because they are like a mule, that is, they are unable to produce new interpretations or cannot be confronted with the traditions of the previous interpretations".

Taking Barthes's theory a step further, Eco argued that meaning is produced not only in the interaction between reader and text, but also, and perhaps more importantly, in the interaction between readers. This is an argument closely associated with another theorist, Stanley Fish, who is one of the most prominent figures in what is known as "reader-response theory". Fish places a lot of emphasis on the interpretative community, explaining how a reader brings into the text a set of criteria, values, assumptions and reading procedures, and that it is those qualities which may act as a guarantee against unlimited interpretation. When Quoyle arrives in Newfoundland, he has to learn a new set of codes, ways of behavior and communication which help him to become a fully integrated member of society. Without that shared knowledge, he would remain a baffled outsider, and just as he has to learn how to "read" his new home in order to participate in its life, so we the readers have to learn how to decipher the novel. The language, syntax and structure create a text that is difficult to read at first, but as we ease into it and learn to understand its intricacies, we are repeating or sharing Quoyle's own journey of self-discovery.

Keeping those theories in mind, we can explore how the novel allows for different readings and different interpretations of events. As we have already seen, the narrative relies on the technique of delayed decoding to create a sense of mystery and strangeness. Because of the complexities of the plot structure, the atmosphere of mystery and intrigue is likely to be more prominent on a first reading. A second reading, however, not only allows a greater appreciation of the writer's skill, but it also makes it easier to appreciate the humour of the text and notice more closely the light-hearted passages and episodes which relieve the sense of sadness and doom that seems to accompany so much of the protagonist's life. In interviews, Proulx may have suggested that the "happy ending" was imposed on an otherwise "unhappy" narrative, but a closer look at the novel allows the reader to see exactly how she gradually builds up to the final union between Quoyle and Wavey.

Their first meeting shows little promise. All Quoyle can tell Billy Pretty is this: " 'She has very good posture,' said Quoyle. Tried to cancel the stupid remark. 'What I mean is, she has a good stride. I mean, tall. She seems tall.' Man Sounds Like Fatuous Fool. In a way he could not explain she seized his attention" (p. 115). Later, Wavey tells Quoyle about her son's condition, and the battles she has fought to give him an education. "What else", Quoyle thinks, "could kindle this heat" (p. 146). The first time he attempts to "kindle her heat", she tells him about the death of her husband by drowning, and how she thinks of him every time she comes near the shore. He, in turn, is reminded of Petal, who is "like an injected vaccine against the plague of love. What was the point of touching Wavey's dry hand?" (p. 195). However, soon after he has realized that Petal's memory is proving destructive, he has an epiphany, a moment of revelation in which, for the first time, he begins to imagine a better future, in a passage worth quoting at some length:

The sharpness of his gaze pierced the past. He saw generations like migrating birds, the bay flecked with ghost sails, the deserted settlements vigorous again, and in the abyss nets spangled with scales. Saw the Quoyles rinsed of evil by the passage of time. He imagined the aunt buried and gone, himself old, Wavey stooped with age, his daughters in faraway lives, Herry still delighted by wooden dogs and colored threads, a grizzled Herry who would sleep in a north room at the top of the house or in the little room under the stairs. A sense of purity renewed, a sense of events in trembling balance flooded him. Everything, everything seemed encrusted with portent. (p. 196)

This passage may be of equal value to readers who accept the love story, happy ending aspect of the novel, and to those who see the development of the relationship as ironic, or at least devoid of romance. Much of the vocabulary and the imagery here revolves around ideas of rebirth and renewal, of new beginnings and a happier future. However, Quoyle also sees death and old age, and Wavey is not assigned a more prominent place than any of the other characters he thinks about; this reading would suggest a happy compromise rather than a love that conquers all. Continuing in the same vein, the narrative then goes on to qualify and add depth and texture to Quoyle's feelings. On page 233, Quoyle begins to feel "something unfolding. But what? Not love, which wrenched and wounded. Not love, which came only once". For much of the novel, Quoyle holds on to the belief that love is passionate and destructive, and that having loved Petal he can never love again. Quoyle "equated misery with love", and "all he felt with Wavey was comfort and a modest joy" (p. 304). However, just as he is forced to reconsider his attitude towards the aunt once he has found out about her traumatic past, so his feelings towards Wavey change when he finds out that her husband was not the good man she cherishes in her memory. Quoyle and Wavey get closer to one another by confessing the pain their previous relationships had caused them, and now for the first time Quoyle begins to wonder whether love "came in other colors than the basic black of none and the red heat of obsession" (p. 309).

The novel's final section, which tells of Quoyle's wedding, begins with an uncharacteristic sentence: "Quoyle experienced moments in all colors, uttered brilliancies, paid attention to the rich sound of waves counting stones, he laughed and wept, noticed sunsets, heard music in rain, said I do" (p. 336). This is untypical in two ways: it is a rare glimpse of happiness in Quoyle's life, but it is also a rare example of a long, full sentence which contrasts sharply with the short, unconnected words or clusters of words that were used to describe his interior life earlier in the book. The language itself, then, seems to be reinforcing the idea that all has ended well, so that when we come to the novel's final sentence, "And it may be that love sometimes occurs without pain or misery", we contrast it with Quoyle's earlier perception of love as a "plague", and can conclude that this is a happy ending.

If we go back a few lines to the top of the paragraph, though, we realize that what the narrator is in fact saying is that "if Jack Buggit could escape from the pickle jar", and "if a bird with a broken neck could fly away", then perhaps love could occur without pain or misery. The bird with the broken neck did not fly away, and while we are asked to accept the "reality" of Jack Buggit's resurrection, its comical implausibility throws into question all our assumptions about a happy ending. The resurrection will strike some readers as forced and out of place; a deeply ironic "happy ending" grafted on to a narrative of very little happiness. Other readers will read it as a metaphor for regeneration and the persistence of family and community ties, and as an affirmation of the fact that in novels as in life there is both comedy and tragedy.

The intermingling of comedy and tragedy, and the various interpretative options that the novel offers, are emphasized in the novel's epigraph which once again comes from *The Ashley Book of Knots*: "In a knot of eight crossings, which is about the average-size knot, there are 256 different "over-and-under" arrangements possible. . . . Make only one change in this "over and under" sequence and either an entirely different knot is made or no knot at all may result". The first time we read the novel, this quotation hardly makes any sense. When we return to it, however, once we have read the novel, we can finally realize its importance: it speaks of narrative strands, permutations and variations, and in so doing it paints a picture of the book it introduces. It warns the readers that this will be a story made up of fragments which have been arranged in a certain manner, but which could equally be rearranged in order to produce different versions of the story. The reader's pleasure lies in tying and untying the knots of this rich, complex narrative.

3

The Novel's Reception

The success and critical acclaim that accompanied the publication of Proulx's first novel, *Postcards*, created both anticipation and reservations as to whether her second novel would live up to the promise of the first one. As it turned out, the reception of *The Shipping News* was even more enthusiastic than that of *Postcards*, and even though the novel was not universally praised, even those critics who expressed reservations about it had to admit that *The Shipping News* left no doubt that Proulx was an accomplished writer.

One thing that nearly all reviewers praised was Proulx's use of language. Writing in *The Spectator*, John Whitworth, one of the few critics who did not take to the novel, conceded that "E. Annie Proulx is obviously a good writer, in the sense that she can make words do what she wants". James Wood of *The Guardian* praised her "daringly poetic" language, while in *The New York Times* Howard Norman noted that "the sinuousness of E. Annie Proulx's prose seems to correspond physically with the textures of the weather and the sea". *The New Republic* critic Verlyn Klinkenborg wrote that as in *Postcards*, in *The Shipping News* Proulx is a "powerfully descriptive writer", while in *Time* magazine John Skow admired "the lash and sting of her language". Different aspects of Proulx's use of language were equally praised: the elliptical language that describes the characters' inner thoughts and feelings; descriptions of landscape, seascape and weather; the author's use of dialogue in creating believable characters, and the delights of her use of Newfoundland dialect. However, many critics also felt that Proulx's language was "too much of a good thing", to quote the *Guardian* reviewer. In *The London Review of Books* Janette Turner Hospital wrote that "the staccato rhythms and stylistic tics prove irritating. Proulx will never use a simple sentence when three end-stopped phrases, punctuated as sentences, will serve", but she had to concede that the book "won her over" all the same.

As we have already seen in Chapter 1, Proulx's novels are always meticulously researched, but the fictional result never seems forced, because the research is transmuted into plausible, coherent worlds that never appear to be contrived. Reviewers of *The Shipping News* picked up on this fact; Howard Norman wrote that "Ms. Proulx is never too showy with her research, though *The Shipping News* is almost an encyclopedia of slang and lore. The way her Newfoundlanders talk, the most factual account seems as high-spirited as gossip over a supper of snow crab, cod cheeks, lobster salad and seal-flipper stew." In *The New Republic*, Klinkenborg also noted that Proulx's research, far from getting in the way of the story, actually enriches it because it saves it from abstraction, without running the risk of ending up in the other extreme of a too well documented, over-determined fictional universe:

Innumerable are the novels that make the human heart an abstract place, without work, without topography, with only the gravity provided by the emotions and the mind brooding upon them. That is not Proulx's way. She is obsessed by what people know about the worlds they inhabit. In *Postcards* you learn from Loyal Blood more that you could imagine wanting to know about how to remove human scent from coyote traps or how to find dinosaur tracks. In *The Shipping News* the subjects are fishing, maritime economy, boat-building, the running of a local newspaper, Canadian politics, yacht upholstery, harbor management and the curious tongue spoken by Newfoundlanders, not to mention knots.

In *World Literature Today*, B. A. St. Andrews made a similar point by noting that "nothing remains unqualified in Proulx country": "*The Shipping News* reaffirms the power of unique idiomatic speech, of characterization, of love, of land- and seascape, and of communion among us."

Reviewers also agreed that the novel was more enjoyable than either *Postcards* or *Heart Songs* because of its lighter tone. The book was described as "vigorous", "witty" and "quirky", and many critics noted that it resembled a fairy tale. John Skow was speaking for many when he wrote that *The Shipping News* is "funnier and kindlier than Proulx's other work", while James Wood affirmed that "Proulx's sense of humour animates the novel, and is one of its most attractive qualities. [. . .] Proulx's book is so funny, so full of delights". However, the mixture of humor and light-heartedness on the one hand and tragedy and gloom on the other left some reviewers not entirely satisfied. Howard Norman felt that Jack Buggit's resurrection was a "forced invention" not in keeping with the rest of the novel's tone, while Klinkenborg also wrote that "in the resurrection of Jack Buggit I found the clearest cause of a reluctance I had been feeling all the way through *The Shipping News*", a reluctance brought on by the fact that, despite the novel being a comedy in which "the tragedy is everywhere", the balance between the two was not quite right.

Proulx's powers of characterization were praised by most critics but, again, some also expressed a few reservations, which were meant to qualify their enthusiasm for the book rather than to suggest any serious failings. Klinkenborg praised Proulx's creation of comic characters, but added that "the characters seem limited, not enlarged, by what goes unspoken". A similar view was expressed in the *Times Literary Supplement* by Natasha Walter, who felt that Proulx "never takes them [her characters] on straight, but always seems to be looking down on them and patting their eccentricities on the head". James Wood modified his praise for the author's use of language by pointing out that "one can have too much of a good thing" in the sense that the writing itself "tilts away from her characters. It doesn't modify or deepen them".

Three years after the publication of *The Shipping News*, John Sutherland was reviewing Proulx's *Accordion Crimes* in *The New Republic*. His review began with an assertion of the author's strength, and a question about her future: "The praise for E. Annie Proulx's *The Shipping News* was unanimous and superlative", he wrote, showing that the praise did by far outweigh any criticism. "It won a string of important prizes. But literary history is littered with examples of authors stifled by their own success. When you suddenly find yourself at the top, where do you go?" Sutherland then proceeded to write an enthusiastic review of *Accordion Crimes*, thus answering his own question: having reached the top, it would seem that Proulx is determined to stay there.

4

The Novel's Performance

The *Shipping News* was an immediate success, earning its author three major awards: the National Book Award for Fiction, the *Irish Times* International Fiction Prize, and the Pulitzer Prize for Fiction. Proulx's American publishers had initially printed 20,000 copies of the novel, but the day after the National Book Award was announced they went back to press for an extra 25,000 copies. As this example illustrates, awards can translate into sales, and they also carry prestige and substantial financial rewards for the author. However, they do not necessarily guarantee popularity with the reading public, nor do they always launch a relatively unknown writer's career. With *The Shipping News*, Annie Proulx reaped all the benefits. The novel spent over forty weeks on *The New York Times* and *Publishers' Weekly* best-seller lists; it has been translated into several languages, and it has become a favorite among reading groups on both sides of the Atlantic. According to a report published in *The Guardian* in March 2001, *The Shipping News* shares fifteenth place with Toni Morrison's *Beloved* in the top twenty of reading groups' favorites. Readers have given the book five stars out of five in British-based internet bookshop Amazon, while in its

American counterpart the novel has earned four stars out of five, based on two hundred and forty readers' reviews.

Sarah Lyall of *The New York Times* interviewed Proulx shortly after the National Book Award was announced, and Proulx said that awards meant "fatter royalty checks, bulkier sacks of fan mail, and a sudden rush of speaking engagements". As we have seen in Chapter 1, such sudden success is a mixed blessing, and Proulx notes that it is not only the demands on her time which may distract her from work, but also the pressure that comes with success. She told Sarah Lyall:

There's also the pressure on future work. It's as if you sewed yourself this incredibly nice suit and it took a lot of care and everywhere you went people said, "This incredible suit—what a knockout". After a while you might start to think of yourself as not just someone who made a pretty good suit but someone with an exalted sense of fashion and exquisite taste, and meanwhile your critics and your admirers just wait for the next suit.

Luckily for both the author and her readers, her subsequent work has indeed confirmed her "exalted sense of fashion". Professor John Sutherland, reviewing *Accordion Crimes* in 1996 wrote: "*Accordion Crimes* uses all the range and the resources of Proulx's mature prose. It is now safe to assert that she is a great novelist. It is a pity she won all those prizes with the last novel [*The Shipping News*]; she deserves to win them again".

In many publications, both in the UK and the USA, *The Shipping News* was chosen as book of the month, book of the year, and recommended book for Christmas in the year of its publication. Its appeal has been wide and varied; it is taught in schools, colleges and universities, and several scholarly articles have already been published, thus earning the novel its place in the literary canon. Meanwhile, the book has also inspired a rock band, who call themselves *The Shipping News* (their website can be found at www.southern.com/southern/band/SHIPN/index2.html). At the time of writing, the novel has been adapted for the cinema by Miramax studios, and is slated for release in the United States on December 25th 2001 and in the UK on March 1st 2002. It has been shot on location in Newfoundland, and has been directed by Lasse Hallström whose recent credits include *The Cider House Rules* and *Chocolat*. The movie stars Kevin Spacey as Quoyle and Dame Judi Dench as the aunt. Other cast members include Julianne Moore, Cate Blanchett and Pete Postlethwaite. Advance word on the movie has been positive, despite its difficult and prolonged production. It will certainly boost sales of Proulx's novel, with the release of a tie-in edition and mass market paperback that will bring *The Shipping News* to a new and wider audience.

In 1999, Princeton academic and feminist critic Elaine Showalter nominated Proulx as "artist of the year" and "new woman of the millennium". As predictions go, hers wasn't a bad one.

Tomoxifen Follow along?

· 5

Further Reading and Discussion *Questions*

1. Many readers do not take to Quoyle from the beginning of the novel. Proulx certainly begins by painting the picture of an unappealing character, and throughout the book she does not let us forget that he is overweight, unattractive, and socially awkward. How does the text invite us to begin to sympathize with Quoyle, and how does his character develop as the narrative unfolds?

2. John Sutherland, reviewing *Accordion Crimes* in *The New Republic*, noted that when we read *The Shipping News*, or indeed any of Proulx's books, we cannot easily discern the influence of other writers past or present. What problems does this create for the reader, and how does it affect our appreciation of the novel?

3. And even though Proulx does not much resemble other contemporary American writers, are there themes and techniques that we can identify as typical of contemporary American fiction?

4. *The Shipping News* is narrated in fragments, and written in a jumpy, elliptical style. How does this affect our aesthetic appreciation of the text? Does the difficulty detract from our reading

pleasure? And how does the narrative style relate to the novel's themes?

5. Natasha Walter, reviewing the novel in the *Times Literary Supplement*, felt that Petal Bear could have been disposed of in a less spectacular and violent way. Do you agree that some details of the plot are unnecessarily exaggerated or unrealistic?

6. We saw in Chapter 1 that Proulx is not happy with the "women's writing" label. Is our understanding of the book in any way enriched by the knowledge that it was written by a female author?

7. In Chapter 38, Bunny has a dream in which the ancestral home is destroyed. She wakes up "mad with fear", but within minutes she is calm again and cannot remember her dream. Discuss the symbolism of this episode. What does it suggest about families, generations, the past and the future?

8. *The Shipping News* explores the political through the personal. Looking at individual characters in the book, what political or ideological issues do you think are raised in relation to them? (For instance, consider Wavey and the support groups she has to set up, or the care available to Cousin Nolan).

9. In Chapter 4, as the ship approaches Newfoundland, the aunt wonders "which had changed most, place or self?" Does the subsequent narrative allow her to find an answer to that question and, more generally, how are setting and character related in the novel?

SUGGESTIONS FOR FURTHER READING

Books by Annie Proulx:

Postcards, London: Flamingo, 1994.
The Shipping News, London: Fourth Estate, 1994.
Heart Songs, London: Fourth Estate, 1996.
Accordion Crimes, London: Fourth Estate, 1997.
Close Range, London: Fourth Estate, 2000.

Articles by Annie Proulx:

"Books on Top", *The New York Times*, 26 May 1994.
"Tell it Like a Person", *The Observer*, 15 June 1997.
"Big Skies, Empty Places", *The New Yorker*, 25 December 2000.

Articles on *The Shipping News*:

Marilyn Babineau. "E. Annie Proulx's *The Shipping News*: A Newfound-
    land Perspective by Stuart Pierson", *Newfoundland Studies* 11, 1, 1995.
Louise Flavin. "Quoyle's Quest: Knots and Fragments as Tools of Narration
    in *The Shipping News*", *Critique*, 40, No 3 (Spring 1999), 239–47.
Vicky Greenbaum. "Beyond the Bookroom: Modern Literature, Modern
    Literacy, and the Teaching of E. Annie Proulx's *The Shipping News*",
    English Journal, 86, No 8 (1997), 17–20.
Tracy Petterson. "Knots and Metaphors in *The Shipping News*", *Notes on
    Contemporary Literature*, 27, No 2 (March 1997), 2–3.
Robert Scott Stewart. "Tayloring the Self: Identity, Articulation, and Com-
    munity in Proulx's *The Shipping News*," *Studies in Canadian Literature*,
    23, No 2 (1998), 49–70.

A book-length scholarly study of Proulx's work was published as this book
    was going to press: Karen L. Rood, *Understanding E. Annie Proulx*,
    University of South Carolina Press, 2001.

Interviews with Annie Proulx and author profiles may be found in magazines as well as on the internet. The following have been consulted and quoted from in this book:

Interviews

Katie Bolick. "Imagination Is Everything", *The Atlantic Monthly*, 12 November 1997.

Sara Rimer Vershire. "At Home with E. Annie Proulx", *The New York Times*, 23 June 1994.

Katharine Viner. "Death and the Author", *The Guardian*, 6 June 1997.

Ros Wynne-Jones, "Happier to Write Than Love", *The Independent*, 1 June 1997.

Internet sites

<www.annieproulx.com.>.
This is the author's official website.

<www.bbc.co.uk/education/bookcase>.
This site contains information on *The Shipping News*, and the transcript of a radio interview.

<www.simonandschuster.com/author.cfm?isbn=0671510053>.
This is the official site of Proulx's publishers, and it contains information on her life and works.

<www.centralbooking.com/authors/proulx/index.htm>.
Another site with useful resources, including biographical details, quotes from interviews, bibliography and links to other sites of interest.

<http://134.153.160.118/educ4142/proulx.htm>.
Despite its unpromising address, this site contains useful links relating to Proulx.

<http://tinpan.fortunecity.com/country/411/annie.html>.
Go to this address for information on Proulx and, best of all, links
to sites on Newfoundland. You will find historical and geographical
information, pictures, and there's even a link to the *Dictionary of
Newfoundland English.*

Book reviews

The following reviews have been used in this book:

David Bradley. "A Family Running on Empty", *The New York Times*, 22
   March 1992.
John DeMont. "An Epiphany on the Rock", *Maclean's*, 25 April 1994.
Verlyn Klinkenborg. "The Princess of Tides", *The New Republic*, 30 May
   1994.
Christopher Lehmann-Haupt. "Lechery and Loneliness in the Hazardous
   West", *The New York Times*, 12 May 1999.
Sarah Lyall. "Book Notes", *The New York Times*, 22 December 1993.
Howard Norman. "In Killick-Claw, Everybody Reads the Gammy Bird",
   The New York Times, 4 April 1994.
Elaine Showalter. "Annie Proulx", *City Pages*, 22 December 1999.
John Skow. "True (as in Proulx) Grit Wins", *Time*, 29 November 1993.
B. A. St. Andrews. 'World Literature in Review', *World Literature Today*,
   69, No 2 (Spring 1995).
John Sutherland. "The Long Journey", *The New Republic*, 7 October 1996.
Janette Turner Hospital. "How to Make Seal-flipper Pie", *The London
   Review of Books*, 10 February 1994.
Natasha Walter. "Newfoundland Kisses", *The Times Literary Supplement*,
   26 November 1993.
John Whitworth. "Was Love then a Bag of Sweets?", *The Spectator*, 4
   December 1993.
James Wood. "Full Steam to Newfoundland", *The Guardian*, 7 November
   1993.

General Reading

The following books were used in Chapter 2:

Roland Barthes. *The Pleasure of the Text,* trans. Richard Miller, Oxford: Blackwell, 1990.

Roland Barthes. "The Death of the Author", in *Image-Music-Text,* trans. Stephen Heath, London: Fontana, 1977.

Malcolm Bradbury. *The Modern American Novel,* Oxford: Oxford University Press, 1992.

Umberto Eco. *Interpretation and Overinterpretation,* Cambridge: Cambridge University Press, 1992.

Stanley Fish. *Is There a Text in This Class?,* Cambridge, MA: Harvard University Press, 1980.

Kenneth Millard. *Contemporary American Fiction: An Introduction to American Fiction Since 1970,* Oxford: Oxford University Press, 2000.

Philip Roth. "Writing American Fiction" in Malcolm Bradbury, ed. *The Novel Today,* London: Fontana, 1990.